REVISED STUDENT EDITION

PLAY and PLAY

Piano Book For Beginners

Written by Diane Engle

© 2016, 2021, 2023 by Diane Engle. Second Edition.
Library of Congress PAu 3-840-092
All rights reserved.
No part of this book may be reproduced in any form or by any electronic or mechanical means, including information storage and retrieval systems, without permission in writing from the author.

dianeengle52@gmail.com
Diane Engle
107 S. Holly Street
DeQuincy, LA 70633
USA

www.dianeenglepianostudio.com

Illustrator: Peggy Condon
Editor: Lindy Robertson
Pre-Press Production: Julie Karen Hodgins

PLAY AND PLAY
Piano Book for Beginners

This book belongs to

_____

Student Edition

I CLIMBED UP THE APPLE TREE

INSTRUCTIONS
Touch each apple as you say the poem.
Color the apples and the apple tree.

Play and Play Piano Book for Beginners

HEARTBEAT CHART

INSTRUCTIONS
Touch each heartbeat as your teacher plays the drum.
Touch each heartbeat as you say the poem.

FIVE FINGER NUMBERS

Trace your hands. Number the fingers.

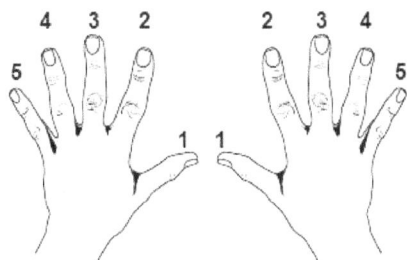

Right hand

Left hand

PIANO KEYBOARD

INSTRUCTIONS
Circle the two black key group.
Find a group of two black keys on the keyboard with your left hand. Use fingers 2 and 3 to play the black keys in the two black key group.
Find a group of two black keys on the keyboard with your right hand. Use fingers 2 and 3 to play the black keys in the two black key group.

Circle the three black key group.
Find a group of three black keys on the keyboard with your left hand. Use fingers 2, 3, and 4 to play the black keys in the three black key group.
Find a group of three black keys on the keyboard with your right hand. Use fingers 2, 3, and 4 to play the black keys in the three black key group.

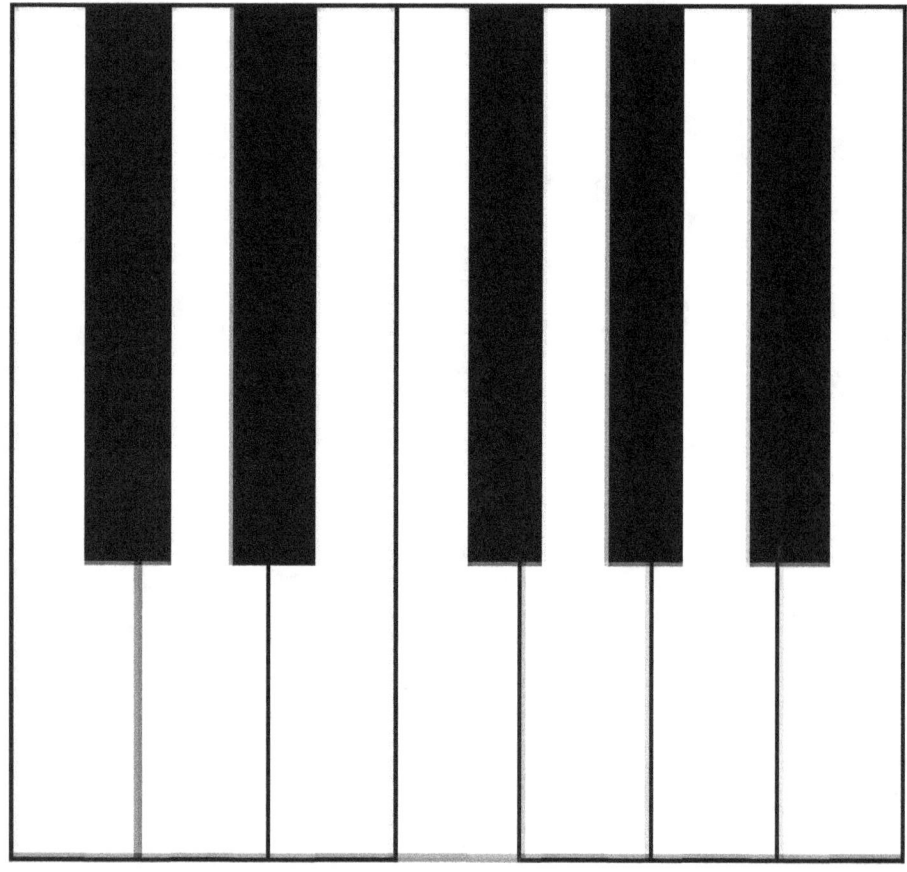

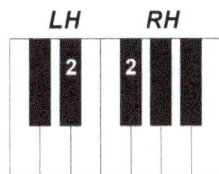

IN AND OUT

INSTRUCTIONS
Put your right hand finger 2 on the group of **three** black keys. Put your left hand finger 2 on the **group of two** black keys. Play with your right hand when finger 2 is above the bean bag. Play with your left hand when finger 2 is below the bean bag.
The heartbeat with no picture means a silent heartbeat. Do not play. Just nod your head on the silent heartbeat.
Play and sing the words.
Color the bean bags.

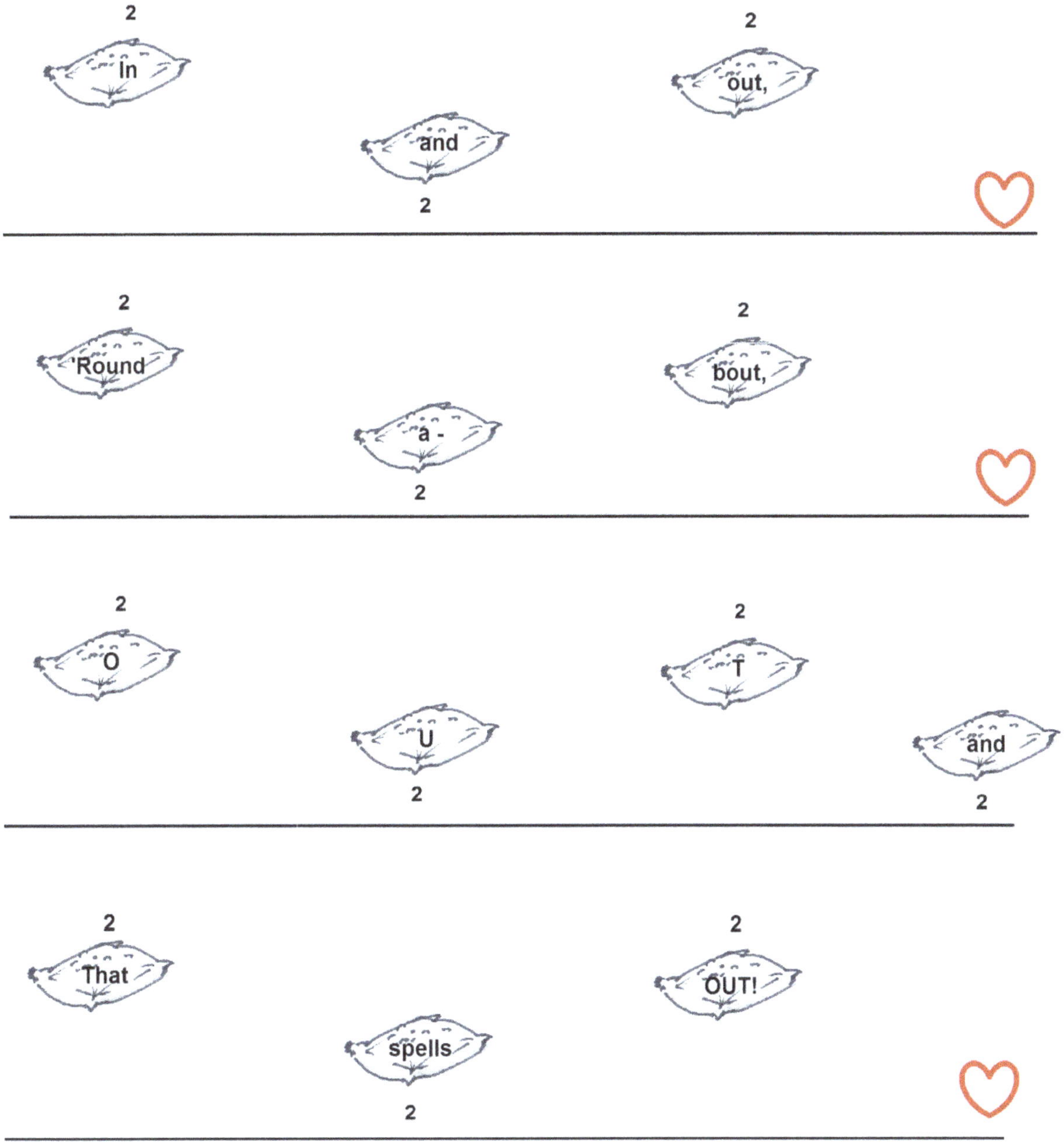

In and out,
Round a- bout,
O U T and
That spells OUT!

Play and Play Piano Book for Beginners

SNAIL, SNAIL

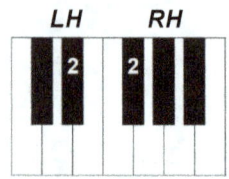

INSTRUCTIONS
Put your right hand finger 2 on the group of three black keys.
Put your left hand finger 2 on the group of two black keys.
Play and sing the finger numbers.
Play and sing the words. Your teacher will help you sing the words under the under the snail picture.

♥ ♥ ♥ ♥

2   2
Snail,   snail,

2   2
snail,   snail,

♥   ♥   ♥   ♥
Go a -   round and   'round and   'round.

Student Edition

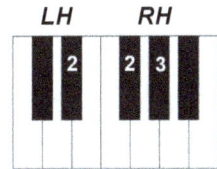

BOUNCE HIGH

INSTRUCTIONS
Put your right hand on a group of three black keys.
Put your left hand on a group of two black keys.
Play and sing the finger numbers.
Remember to play with your right hand when the finger numbers are above the picture and with your left hand when the finger numbers are below the picture.
Play and sing the words.

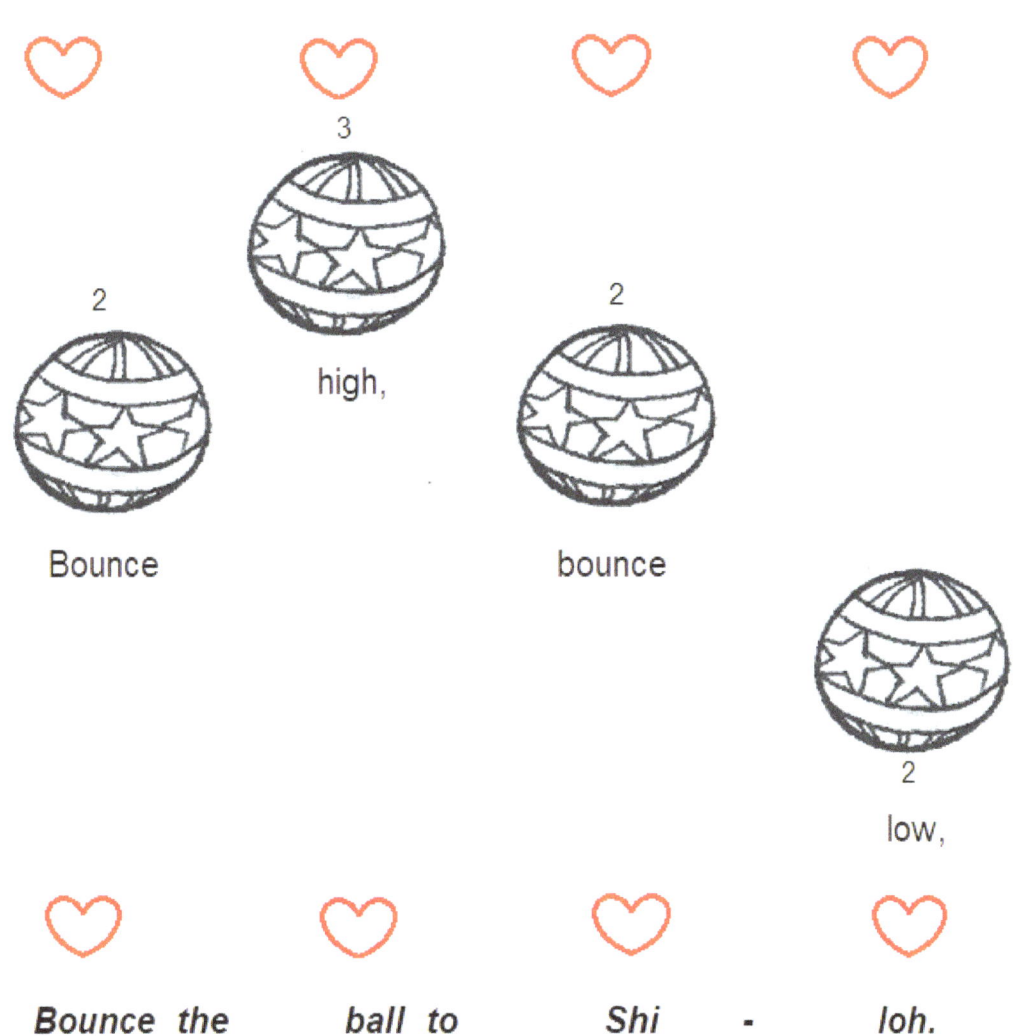

APPLE, PEACH, PEAR, PLUM

INSTRUCTIONS
Say the poem and clap the way the words go.
Touch the pictures and say the poem. Be sure to touch each picture.
Touch the pictures and say the long and short-short sounds.
Clap and say the long and short-short sounds.

Ap · ple,   peach,   pear,   plum;

Tell me   when your   birth- day   comes.

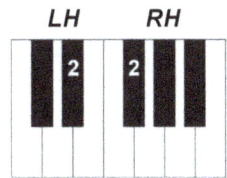

RAIN, RAIN

INSTRUCTIONS

Clap and read the long and short-short sounds.
Put your right hand finger 2 on a group of three black keys.
Put your left hand finger 2 on a group of two black keys.
Play with your right hand when 2 is above the raindrop picture.
Play with your left hand when 2 is below the raindrop picture.
Play and sing the long and short-short sounds then play and sing the words.
Touch your head with your fingertips as you sing the bottom line of words.

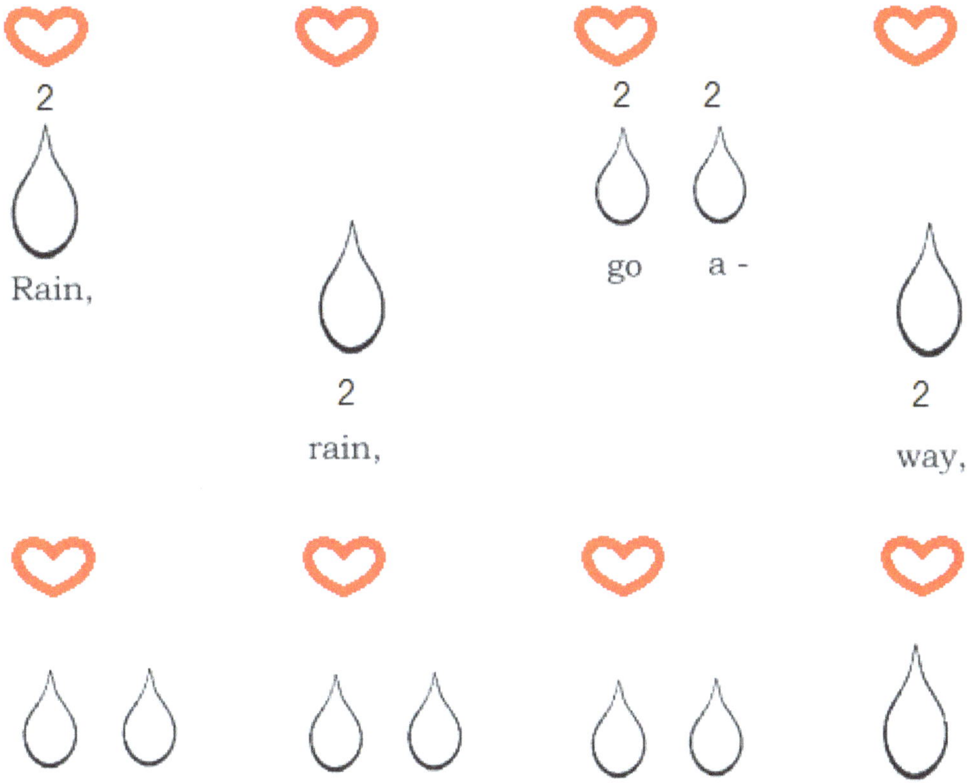

♥   ♥   ♥   ♥   ♥

2   2   2

Rain,   rain,   go a-   way,
         2   2

♥   ♥   ♥   ♥

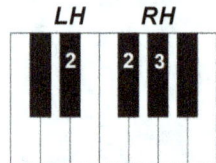

BOUNCE HIGH

INSTRUCTIONS
Touch the pictures and say the long and short-short sounds.
Clap and read the long and short-short sounds.
Put your right hand on the group of three black keys.
Put your left hand on the group of two black keys.
Play and sing the long and short-short sounds then play and sing the words.

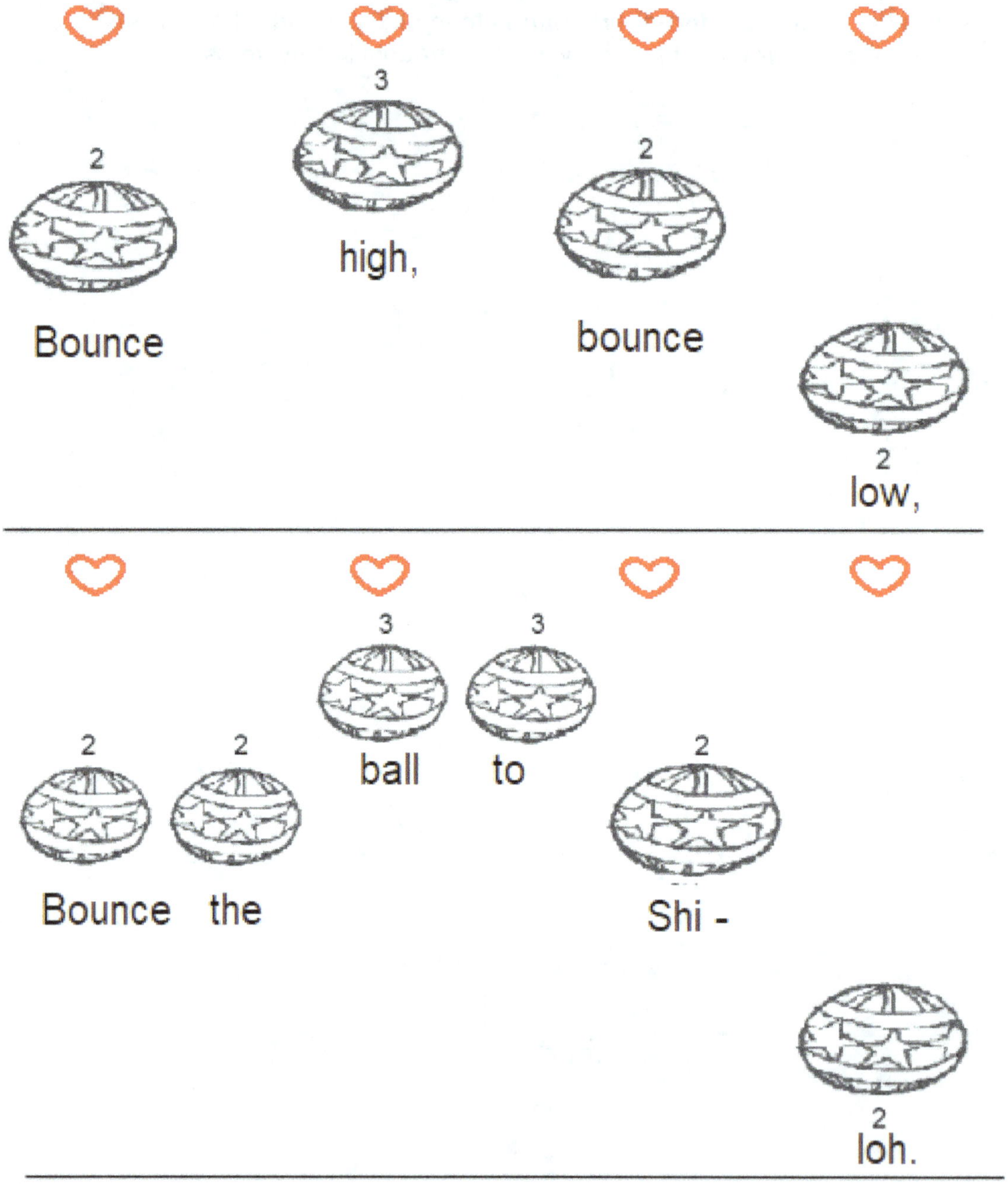

Bounce high, bounce low,

Bounce the ball to Shi - loh.

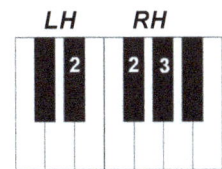

LUCY LOCKET

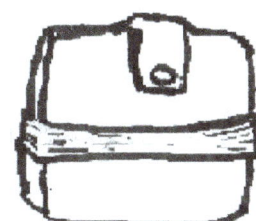

INSTRUCTIONS
Clap and read the long and short-short sounds.
Put your right hand on a group of three black keys and your left hand on a group of two black keys.
Play and sing the finger numbers then play and sing the long and short-short sounds.
Play and sing the words.

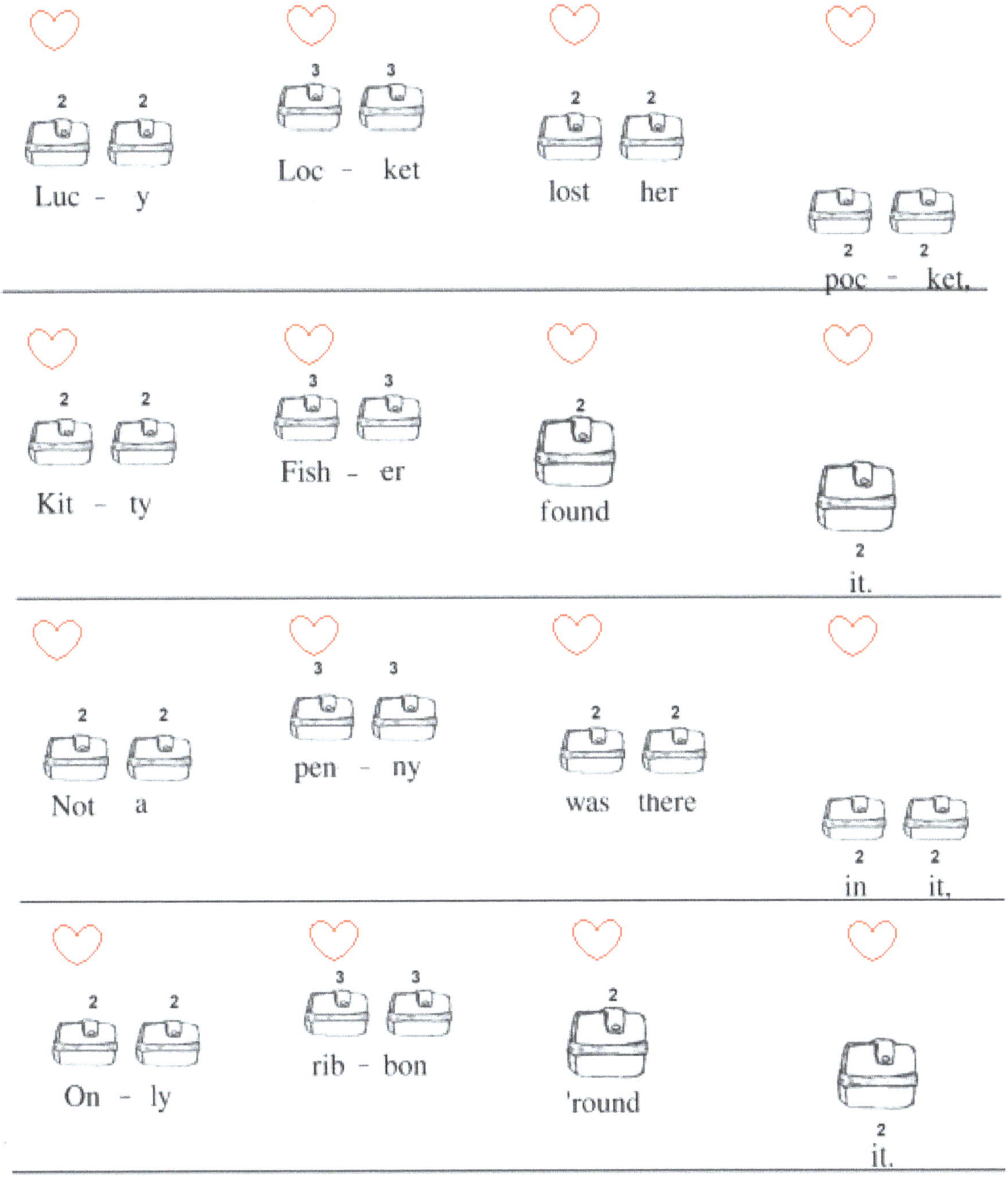

Luc - y   Loc - ket   lost her   poc - ket.

Kit - ty   Fish - er   found   it.

Not a   pen - ny   was there   in it,

On - ly   rib - bon   'round   it.

Play and Play Piano Book for Beginners

APPLE, PEACH, PEAR, PLUM

INSTRUCTIONS
Touch each heartbeat as you say the poem.
Touch each word or part of the word as you say the poem.
Clap the rhythm as you say the poem. Remember, the rhythm is *"the way the words go."*
Clap and read the rhythm names.

BEE, BEE, BUMBLEBEE

INSTRUCTIONS
Touch each heartbeat as you say the poem.
Touch each word or part of the word as you say the poem.
Clap the rhythm as you say the poem. Remember, the rhythm is *"the way the words go."*
Clap and read the rhythm note names.

Bee, Bee, Bum - ble Bee,

Stung a man up - on his knee.

Stung a pig up - on his snout.

I de - clare if you aren't out!

Play and Play Piano Book for Beginners

PEASE PORRIDGE HOT

INSTRUCTIONS
Pat the beat as you read the words.
Clap the rhythm as you read the words. Remember, the rest is a silent beat.
Clap and read the rhythm note names.

♩	♫	♩	𝄽
Pease	por- ridge	hot,	

♩	♫	♩	𝄽
Pease	por- ridge	cold.	

♩	♫	♫	♩
Pease	por- ridge	in the	pot,

♩	♩	♩	𝄽
Nine	days	old.	

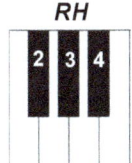

CLOSET KEY

INSTRUCTIONS
Touch the heartbeats and read the rhythm.
Touch the notes and read the rhythm.
Clap and read the rhythm.
Put your right hand on the group of three black keys.
Play and sing the finger numbers.
Play and sing the rhythm names then play and sing the words.

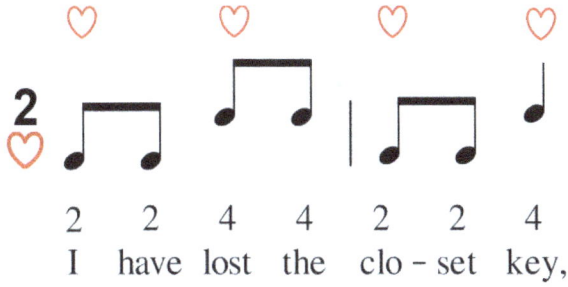

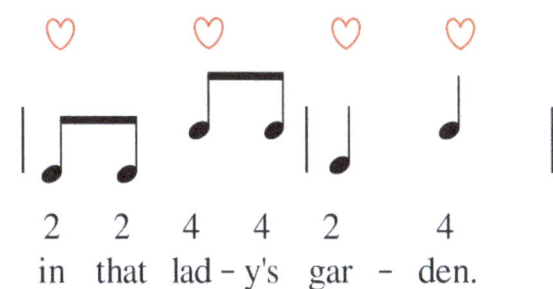

```
2    2    4    4    2    2    4         2    2    4    4    2         4
I    have lost the  clo- set  key,      in   that lad- y's  gar   -   den.
```

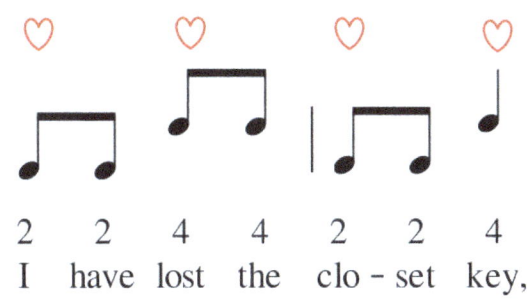

```
2    2    4    4    2    2    4         2    2    4    4    3         2
I    have lost the  clo- set  key,      In   that lad- y's  gar   -   den.
```

Play and Play Piano Book for Beginners

LH
4 3 2

FROG IN THE MEADOW

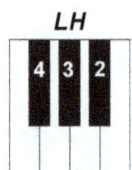

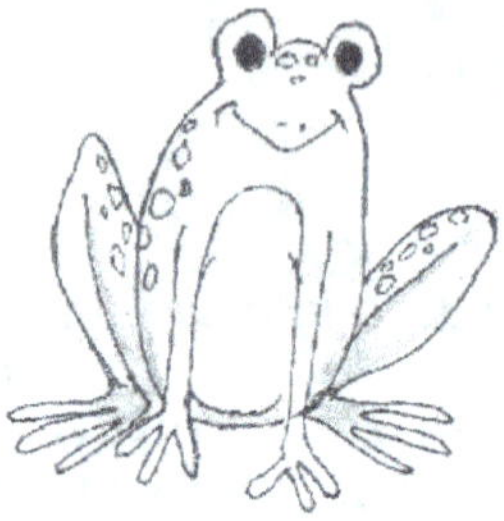

INSTRUCTIONS
Touch the heartbeats and read the rhythm.
Touch the notes and read the rhythm.
Clap and read the rhythm.
Put your left hand on the group of three black keys.
Play and sing the finger numbers.
Play and sing the rhythm names then play and sing the words.

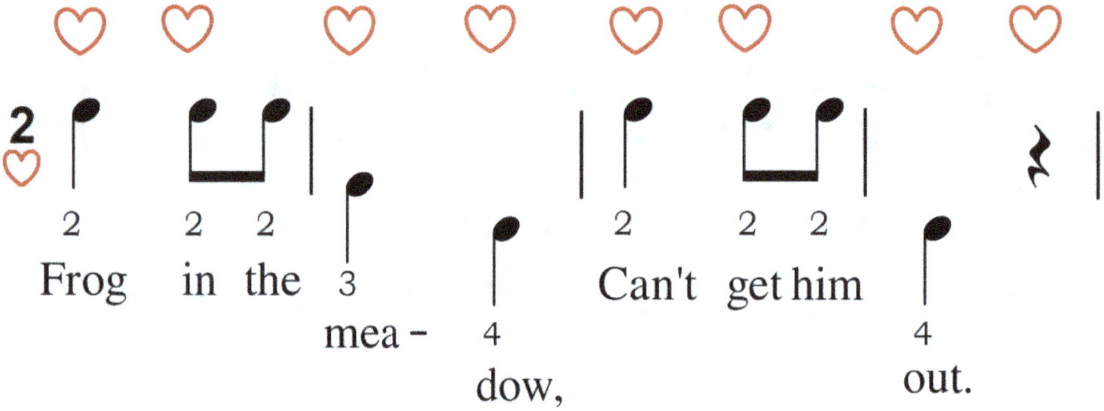
2
2 2 2 3 4 2 2 2 4
Frog in the mea - dow, Can't get him out.

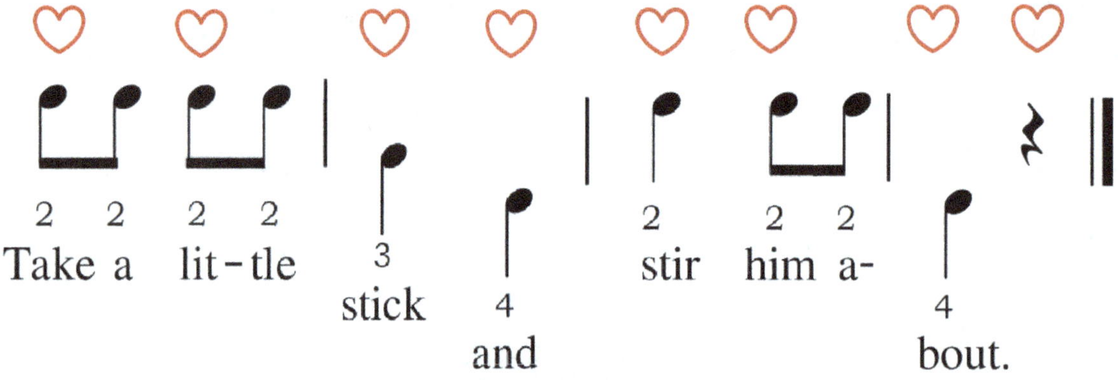
2 2 2 2 3 4 2 2 2 4
Take a lit - tle stick and stir him a- bout.

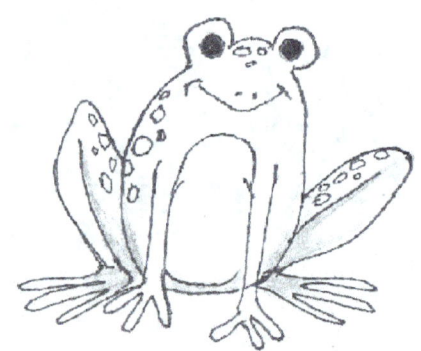

MUSIC ALPHABET

INSTRUCTIONS

The music alphabet is A B C D E F G. The music alphabet gives each white key on the piano a letter name.

Write the music alphabet on the line below. Be sure to use capital letters.

_____

Circle the D on the keyboard below. D is the white key in the middle of the two black key group. Play D white key on the keyboard.

Circle the F on the keyboard below. F is the white key touching the first black key in the three black key group. Play F white key on the keyboard.

Put your right hand second finger on D and your right hand fourth finger on F. Play D then F. Now play F then D. What note name did you skip? Which finger did you skip?

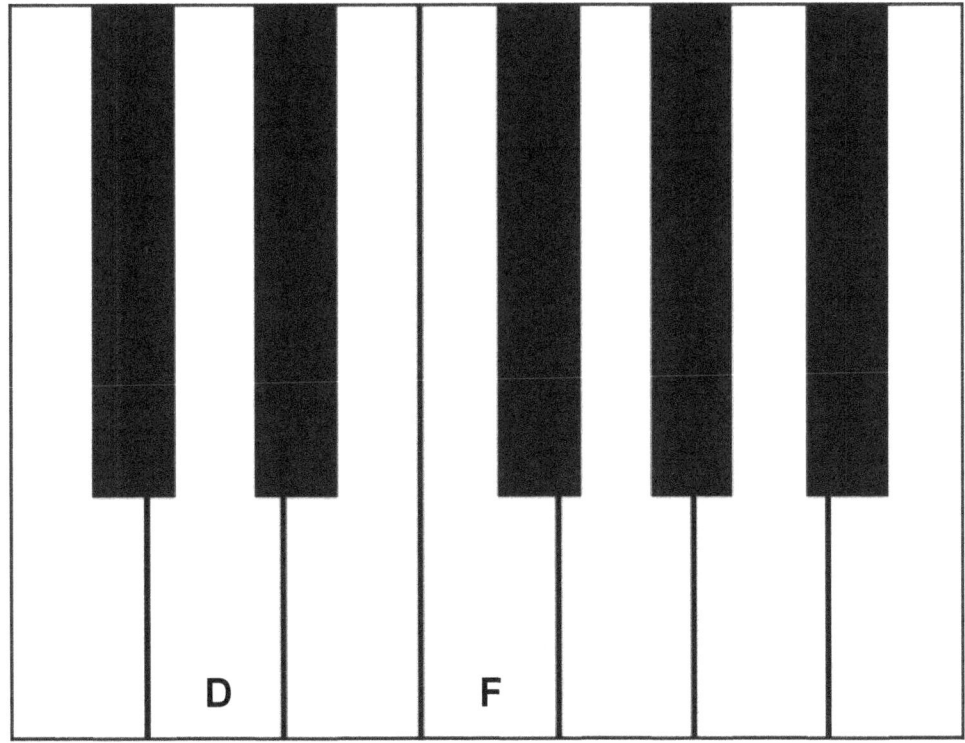

Play and Play Piano Book for Beginners

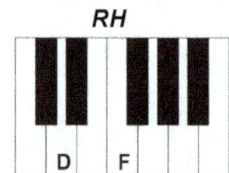

DOGGIE, DOGGIE

INSTRUCTIONS
Clap and read the rhythm.
Put finger 4 of your right hand on the F white key. F white key touches the first black key in the group of 3 black keys.
Finger 2 will play the D white key. D white key is found in between the black keys of the 2 black key group. Play and sing the letter names.
Play and sing the rhythm names then play and sing the words.

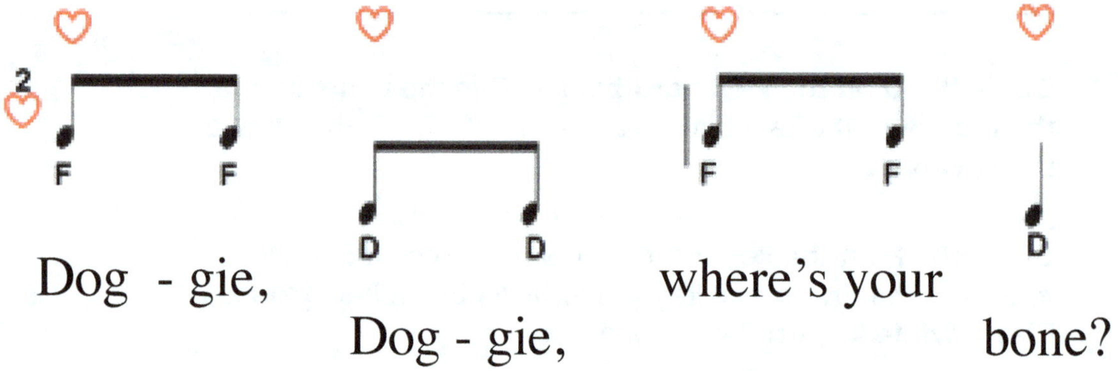

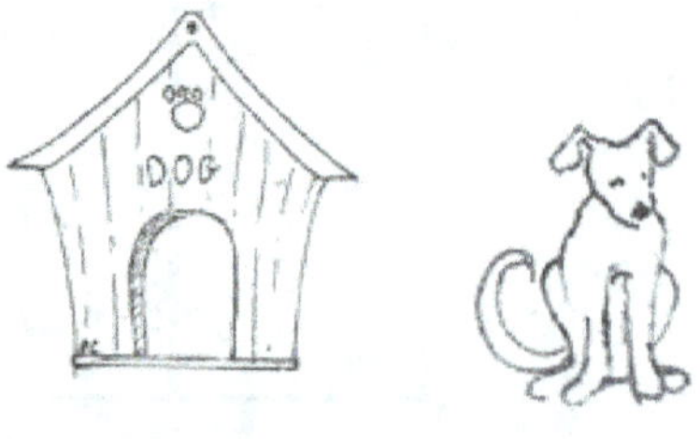

Dog - gie, Dog - gie, where's your bone?

Some-one stole it from your home!

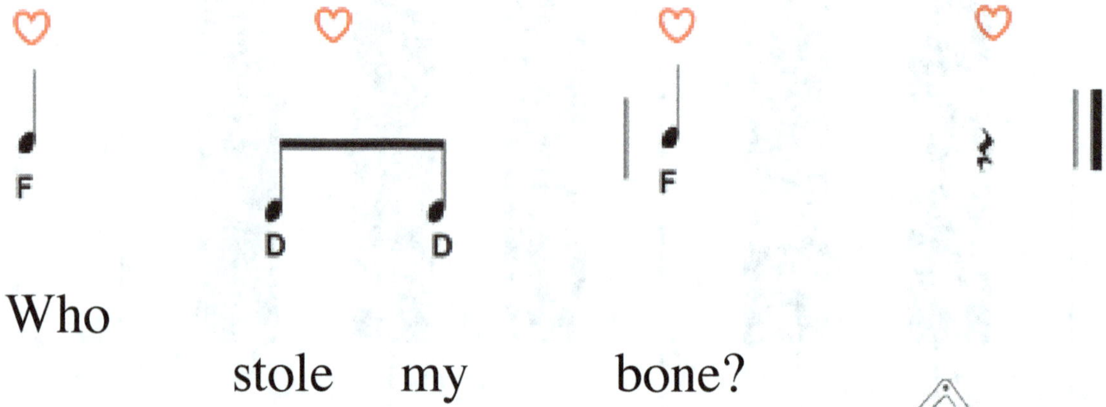

Who stole my bone?

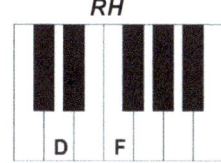

IN AND OUT

INSTRUCTIONS
Clap and read the rhythm.
Put finger 4 of your right hand on the F white key.
Finger 2 will play the D white key.
Play and sing the note names then play and sing the words.

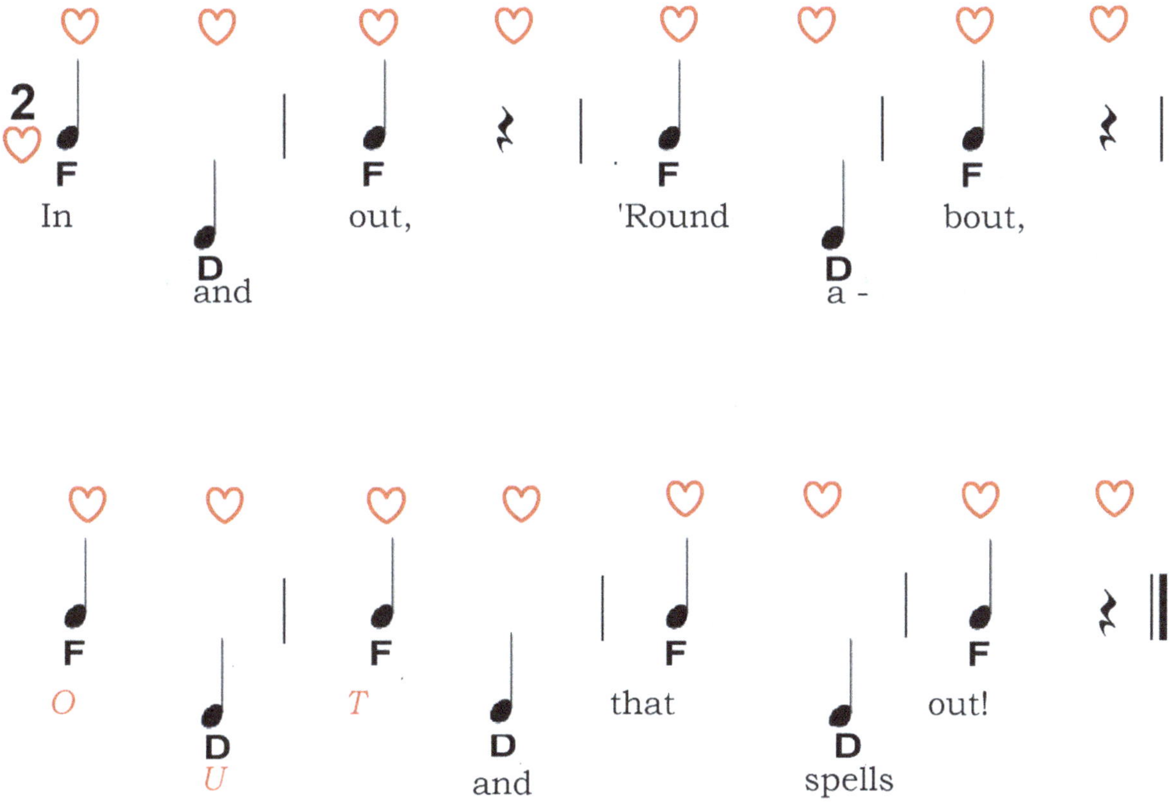

F	F	F	F
In	and out,	'Round	a- bout,
	D		D

F	F	F	F
O	T	that	out!
U	and	spells	
D	D		D

What color are your bean bags?

Play and Play Piano Book for Beginners

MUSIC STAFF

The music staff is where the notes sit. The music staff is made up of lines and spaces.

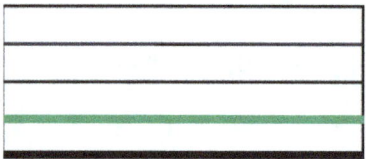

Find these places on the music staff:
- Touch the thick black bottom line with your pencil point. That is line 1.
- Touch the green line above it. That is line 2.
- Touch the space that is found between the bottom black line and the green line. That is space 1.
- Touch the space that is found below the bottom black line. That is called space under the staff.

TREBLE CLEF SIGN

The treble clef sign sits on the music staff. This sign gives each line and space a letter name from the music alphabet.

F is the name of space 1 on the staff. Touch **F** space note with your pencil point.

D is the name of the space under the staff. Touch **D** space note with your pencil point.

Play and sing the notes on the music staff below.

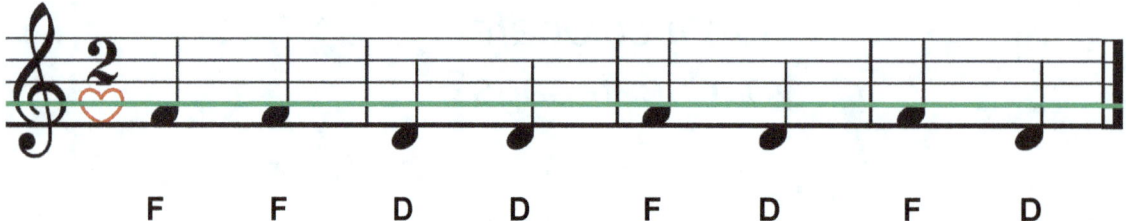

F   F   D   D   F   D   F   D

22 Student Edition

RAIN, RAIN

INSTRUCTIONS
Clap and read the rhythm.
Put finger 4 on F. Remember, F is found in the bottom space of the staff. D is found in the space under the staff.
Play and sing the note names then play and sing the words.

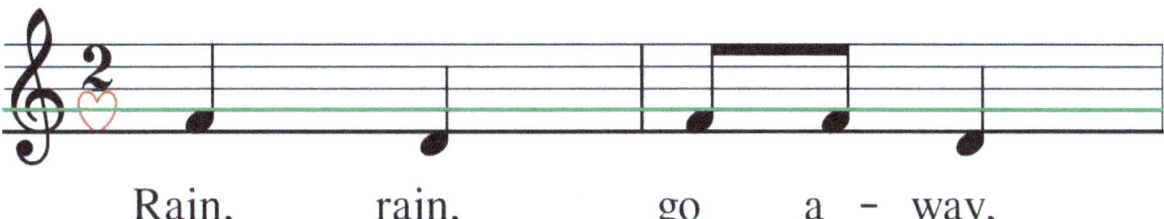

Come again some other day!

Play and Play Piano Book for Beginners

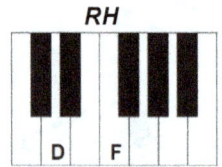

DOGGIE, DOGGIE

INSTRUCTIONS
Clap and read the rhythm.
Put finger 4 of your right hand on F.
Play and sing the note names then play and sing the words.

Dog - gie,   Dog - gie,   where's your   bone?

Someone stole it from your home!

Who   stole   my   bone?

Student Edition

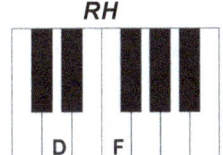

IN AND OUT

INSTRUCTIONS
Clap and read the rhythm.
Put finger 4 of your right hand on F. Finger 2 will play D.
Play and sing the note names, then play and sing the words.

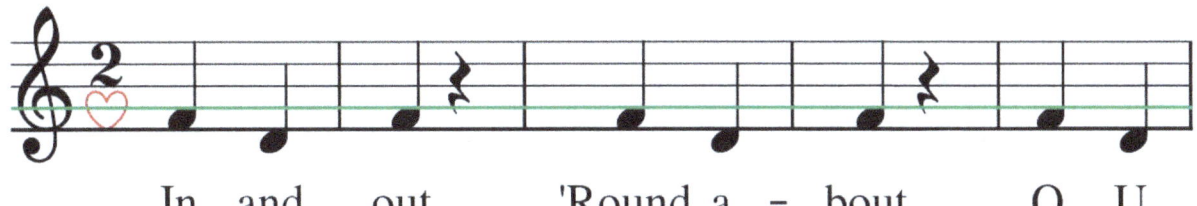

In and out, 'Round a - bout, O U

T and that spells out!

What color are your bean bags?

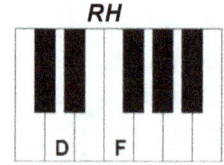

LEMONADE

INSTRUCTIONS
Clap and read the rhythm.
Put finger 4 of your right hand on F.
Play and sing the note names then play and sing the words.
This game song has two parts. It is a conversation. Take turns playing the different parts with your teacher or another student. One part is in red and the other part is in blue.

Here we come!   Where from?   New York.

What's your trade?   Lem-on-ade.   Give us some!   Have none!

Get to work and make us some!

DUCKS AND GEESE

INSTRUCTIONS
Clap and read the rhythm.
Put finger 4 of your right hand on F.
Play and sing the note names then play and sing the words.
Play and sing the words that are in red while your teacher or another student plays and sings the words that are in blue.

Come home all my ducks and geese. No we won't!

Why not? 'Cause not! What's wrong? It's the wolf!

Where's he hid-ing? In the woods. Do-ing what? Wash-ing.

Where's he wash-ing? By the lit-tle riv - er. What's he dry his

hands on?

On the kitty cat's tail!

Play and Play Piano Book for Beginners

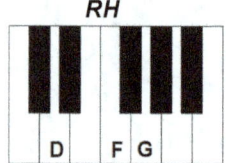

BOUNCE HIGH

INSTRUCTIONS

Touch the notes and read the rhythm.
Clap and read the rhythm.
Put your right hand finger 4 on F. Finger 5 will play G.
Play and sing the note names.
Play and sing the words.

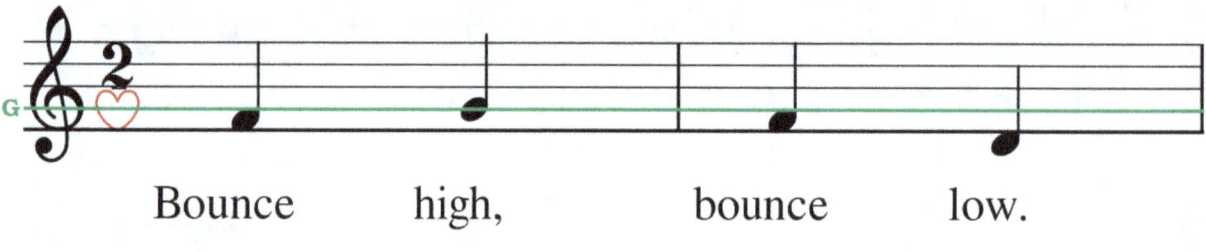

Bounce high, bounce low.

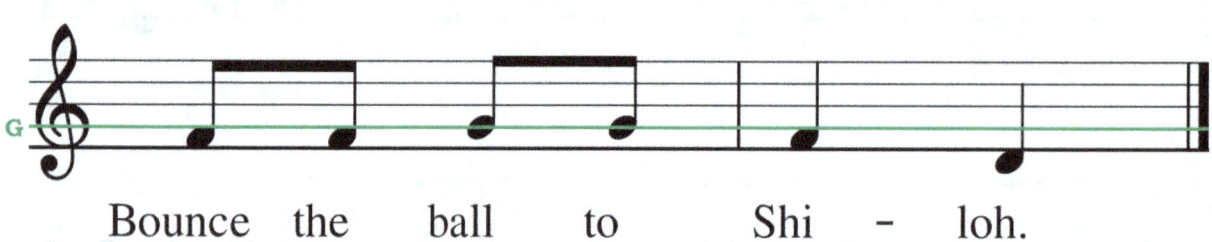

Bounce the ball to Shi - loh.

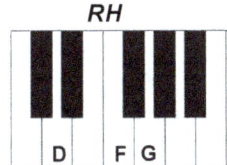

LUCY LOCKET

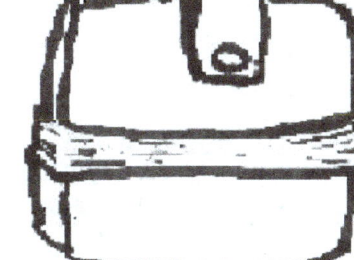

INSTRUCTIONS
Clap and read the rhythm.
Put your right hand finger 4 on F. Finger 5 will play G.
Play and sing the note names then play and sing the words.

Luc - y Loc-ket   lost her poc-ket, Kit-ty Fish-er   found it.

Not a pen-ny   was there in it,   on - ly rib-bon 'round it.

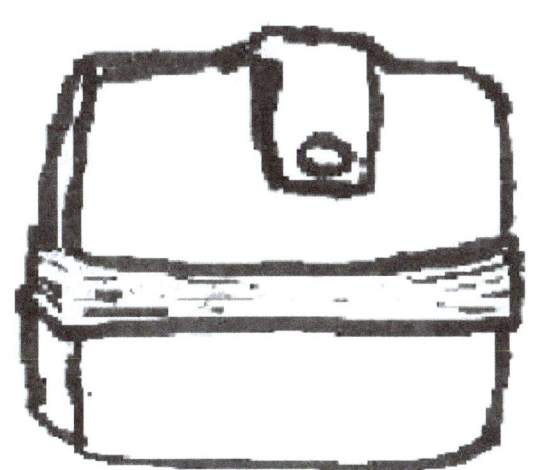

Play and Play Piano Book for Beginners

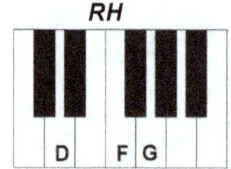

PLAINSIES, CLAPSIES

INSTRUCTIONS
Clap and read the rhythm.
Put your right hand finger 4 on F. Finger 5 will play G.
Play and sing the note names then play and sing the words.

Plain - sies,   clap - sies,   twirl a-round to   back - sies.

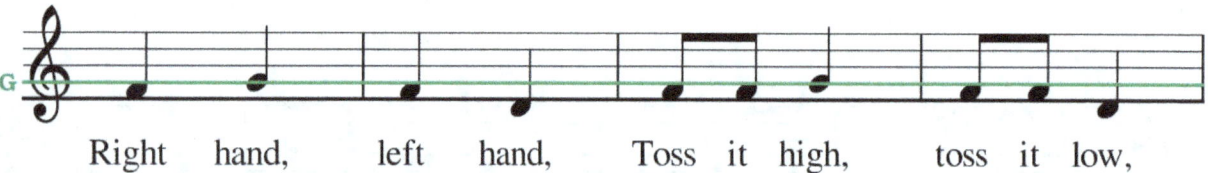

Right   hand,   left   hand,   Toss it high,   toss it low,

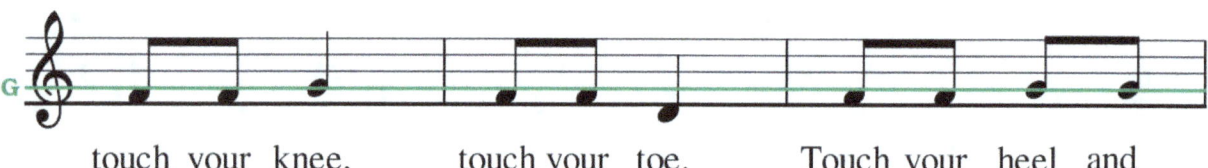

touch your knee,   touch your toe.   Touch your heel and

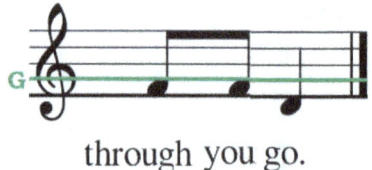

through you go.

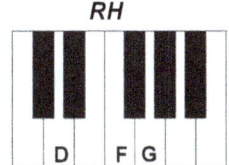

WE ARE DANCING IN THE FOREST

INSTRUCTIONS
Clap and read the rhythm.
Put finger 4 of your right hand on F. Finger 5 will play G.
Play and sing the note names then play and sing the words.

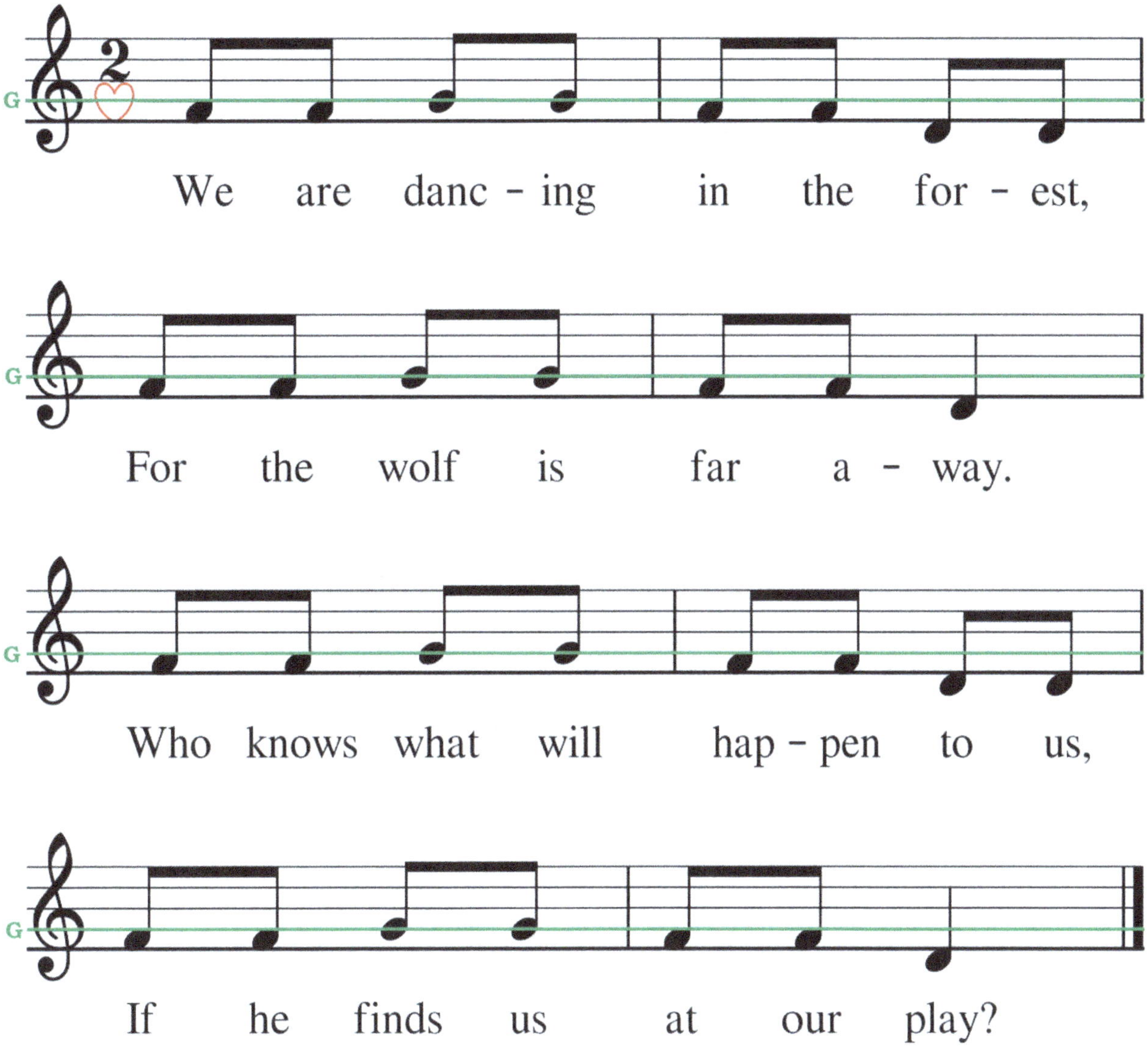

We are danc - ing in the for - est,

For the wolf is far a - way.

Who knows what will hap - pen to us,

If he finds us at our play?

(Spoken) *"Oh Wolf, are you there?"*

Play and Play Piano Book for Beginners

Color the picture of the wolf.

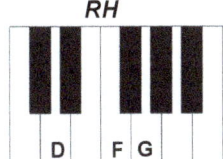

NANNY GOAT

INSTRUCTIONS
Clap and read the rhythm.
Put finger 4 of your right hand on F.
Play and sing the note names. Watch for the jump from D to G.
Play and sing the words.

Nan - ny, Nan - ny   Nan - ny   Goat,

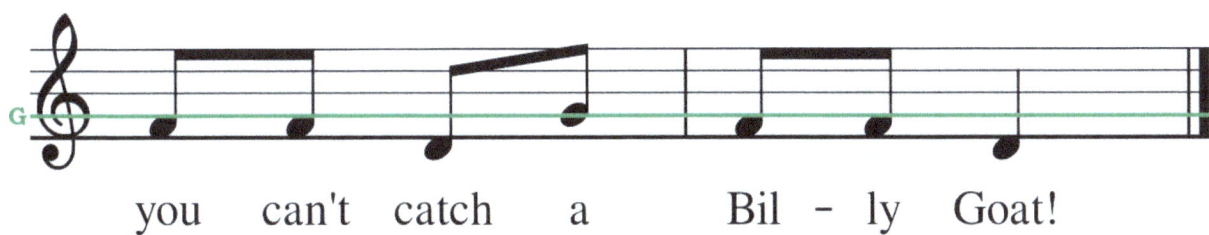

you   can't   catch   a   Bil - ly   Goat!

Play and Play Piano Book for Beginners

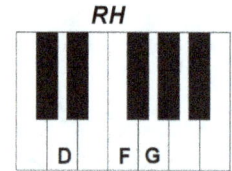

JOHNNY'S IT

INSTRUCTIONS
Clap and read the rhythm.
Put your right hand finger 4 on F. Watch for the jump from D to G.
Play and sing the note names then play and sing the words.

John – ny's it,   he   had a   fit.   He can't do   a –

rith – me – tic.   "Hel – lo,   who am   I?"

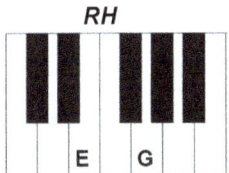

LEMONADE

INSTRUCTIONS
Here is an old game song. It is found in a new place on the staff.
Put finger 5 of your right hand on G. Finger 3 will play E.
Play and sing the note names, then play and sing the words.
Play the different parts as you did before.

Here we come!   Where from?   New York.

What's your trade?   Lem-on-ade.   Give us some!   Have none!

Get to work and make us some!

Play and Play Piano Book for Beginners

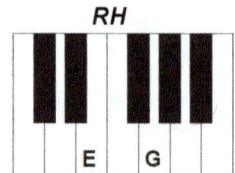

IN AND OUT

INSTRUCTIONS
Here is an old game song. It is found in a new place on the staff.
Put finger **5** of your right hand on G. Finger **3** will play E.
Play and sing the note names then play and sing the words.

In and out, 'Round a - bout,

O U T and that spells out!

What color are your bean bags?

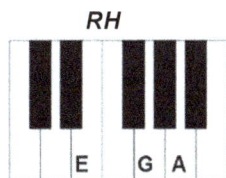

TREBLE CLEF E G A

INSTRUCTIONS
Here are two old songs that have our new note, A.
Clap and read the rhythm of each song.
Put your right hand finger 4 on G. Finger 5 will play A. Finger 2 will play E.
Play and sing the note names then play and sing the words.

BOUNCE HIGH

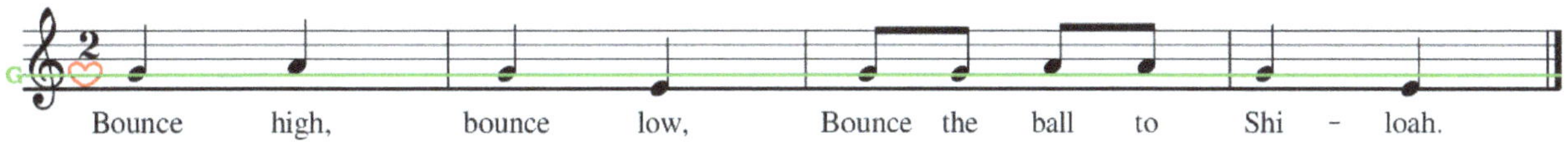

Bounce high, bounce low, Bounce the ball to Shi - loah.

PLAINSIES, CLAPSIES

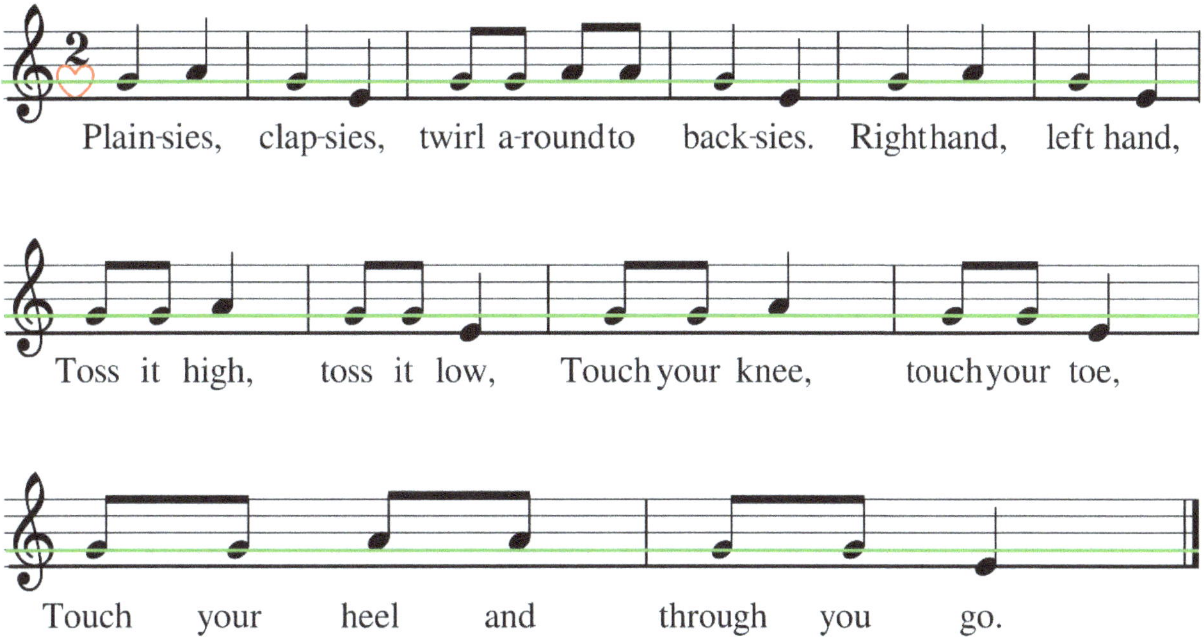

Plain-sies, clap-sies, twirl a-round to back-sies. Right hand, left hand,

Toss it high, toss it low, Touch your knee, touch your toe,

Touch your heel and through you go.

Play and Play Piano Book for Beginners

FROG IN THE MEADOW

INSTRUCTIONS
Here is an old song that uses F G A.
Clap and read the rhythm.
Put your right hand thumb on F. Finger 2 will play G and finger 3 will play A.
Play and sing the letter names then play and sing the words.

Frog in the mea-dow, can't get him out,

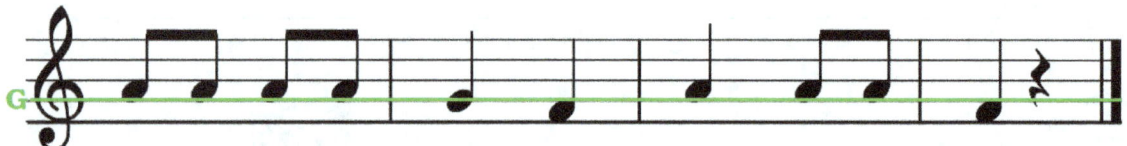

Take a lit-tle stick and stir him a-bout.

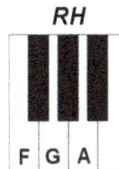

HOP OLD SQUIRREL

INSTRUCTIONS
Clap and read the rhythm.
Put your right hand thumb on F. Finger 2 will play G and finger 3 will play A.
Play and sing the letter names then play and sing the words.

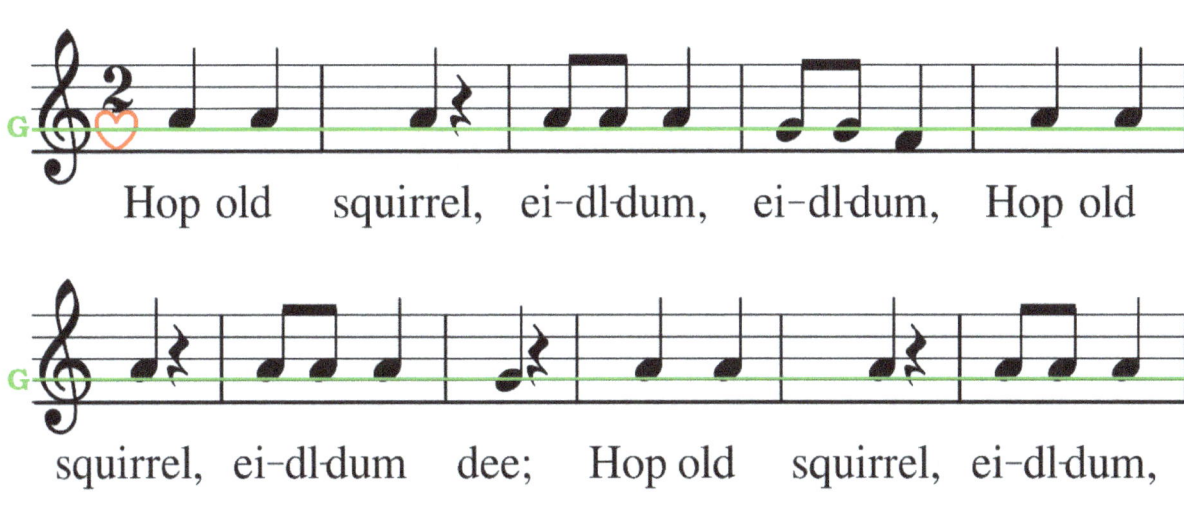

Hop old squirrel, ei-dl-dum, ei-dl-dum, Hop old squirrel, ei-dl-dum dee; Hop old squirrel, ei-dl-dum, ei-dl-dum, Hop old squirrel, ei-dl-dum dee.

Play and Play Piano Book for Beginners

HOT CROSS BUNS

INSTRUCTIONS
Clap and read the rhythm.
Put your right hand thumb on Middle C.
Finger 2 will play D. Finger 3 will play E.
Play and sing the note names then play and sing the words.

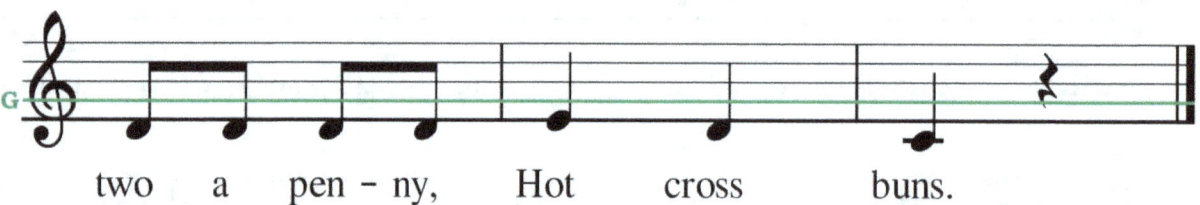

FROG IN THE MEADOW

INSTRUCTIONS
Clap and read the rhythm.
Put your right hand thumb on Middle C.
Finger 2 will play D. Finger 3 will play E.
Play and sing the note names then play and sing the words.

Frog in the mea-dow, can't get him out. Take a lit-tle

stick   and   stir   him a - bout.

Leap, leap, leap, down!

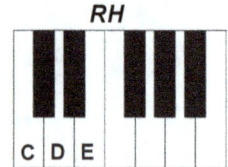

HOP OLD SQUIRREL

INSTRUCTIONS
Clap and read the rhythm.
Put your right hand thumb on Middle C.
Finger 2 will play D. Finger 3 will play E.
Play and sing the note names then play and sing the words.

Hop old squirrel, ei - dl-dum, ei - dl-dum, Hop old

squirrel, ei-dl-dum dee; Hop old squirrel, ei - dl-dum,

ei - dl-dum, Hop old squirrel, ei - dl-dum dee.

CLOSET KEY

INSTRUCTIONS
Clap and read the rhythm.
Put your right hand thumb on Middle C.
Finger 2 will play D. Finger 3 will play E.
Play and sing the note names then play and sing the words.

I have lost the clos-et key, in that lad-y's gar-den.

I have lost the clos-et key, in that lad-y's gar-den.

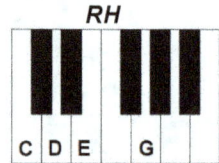

BUTTON, YOU MUST WANDER

INSTRUCTIONS
Clap and read the rhythm.
Put your right hand thumb on Middle C.
Play and sing the note names then play and sing the words.

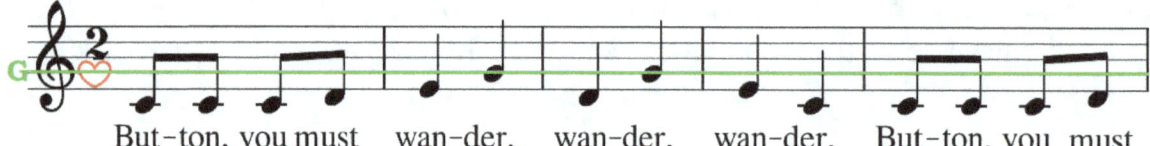

But-ton, you must wan-der, wan-der, wan-der, But-ton, you must

wan-der, ev-'ry-where. Bright eyes will find you, Sharp eyes will

find you, But-ton, you must wan-der ev-'ry-where!

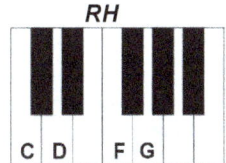

DADDY SHOT A BEAR

INSTRUCTIONS
Clap and read the rhythm.
Put your right hand thumb on Middle C.
Play and sing the name names then play and sing the words.

Dad-dy shot a bear,   Dad-dy shot a bear,

Shot him through the key-hole, and nev-er touched a hair!

Play and Play Piano Book for Beginners

KING'S LAND

INSTRUCTIONS
Clap and read the rhythm.
Put your right hand thumb on Middle C.
Finger 5 will play G and A.
Play and sing the note names then play and sing the words.

I'm on the King's land, the King is not at home.

He's gone to Bos - ton to buy his wife a comb.

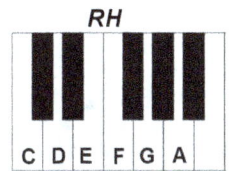

NAUGHTY KITTY CAT

INSTRUCTIONS
Clap and read the rhythm.
Put your right hand thumb on Middle C.
Finger 5 will play G and A.
Play and sing the note names then play and sing the words.

Naugh-ty kit-ty cat, you are ver-y fat! You have but-ter

on your whisk-ers, naugh-ty kit-ty cat! *Scat!*

Play and Play Piano Book for Beginners

RING AROUND THE ROSIE

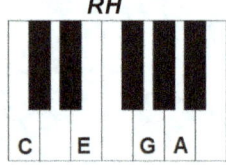

INSTRUCTIONS
Clap and read the rhythm.
Put your right hand thumb on Middle C.
Finger 5 will play G and A.
Play and sing the note names then play and sing the words.

Ring a-round the ros - ie, Poc-ket full of

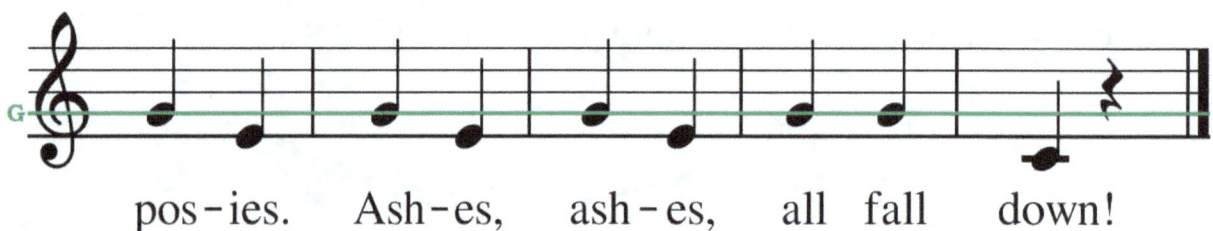

pos - ies. Ash-es, ash-es, all fall down!

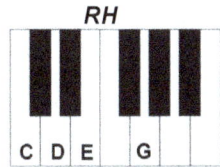

WHO'S THAT TAPPING AT THE WINDOW?

INSTRUCTIONS
Circle the repeat sign.
Circle the half note.
Clap and read the rhythm. Remember to follow the repeat sign.
Put your right hand thumb on Middle C.
Play and sing the rhythm names then play and sing the words.

Who's that tap-ping at the win-dow? Who's that
I am tap-ping at the win-dow, I am

knock-ing at the door?
knock-ing at the door.

Play and Play Piano Book for Beginners

FRÈRE JACQUES

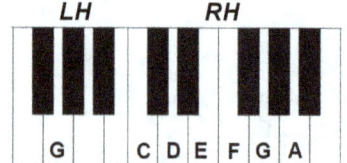

INSTRUCTIONS
Put two dots beside the double bar line to make it a repeat sign.
Clap and read the rhythm.
Put your right hand thumb on Middle C.
Finger 5 will play G and A.
Use your left hand finger 4 to play G that is written below the staff.
It is the G that is lower, or to the left of Middle C.
Play and sing the note names then play and sing the words.
Play and sing the song in a round with your teacher or another student.

Frè - re Jac - ques, Frè - re Jac - ques, Dor - mez vous?

Dor - mez vous? Sonnez les ma - tin - es, Sonnez les ma - tin - es,

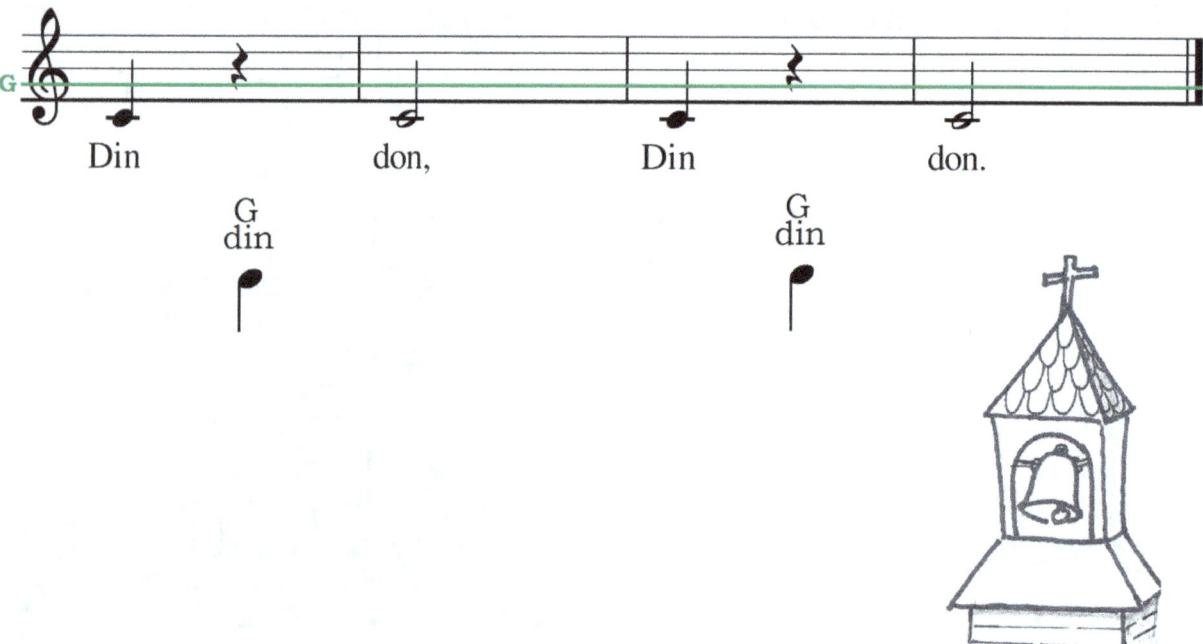

Din don, Din don.

G   G
din din

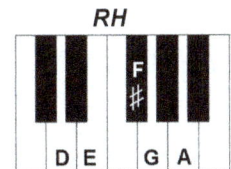

OLD WOMAN

INSTRUCTIONS
Circle all the F#'s in the song.
Clap and read the rhythm.
Put your right hand thumb on D. Finger 3 will play F#.
Play and sing the note names then play and sing the words.

1. Old wo-man, Old wo-man, are you fond of smok-ing?

Old wo-man, Old wo-man, are you fond of smok-ing?

Speak a lit-tle loud-er sir, I'm ver-y hard of hear-ing!

Speak a lit-tle loud-er sir, I'm ver-y hard of hear-ing!

2. Old Woman, Old Woman, are you fond of carding? (repeat)
   Speak a little louder, sir, I'm very hard of hearing! (repeat)

3. Old Woman, Old Woman, don't you want me to court you? (repeat)
   Speak a little louder, sir, I just began to hear you! (repeat)

4. Old Woman, Old Woman, don't you want to marry me? (repeat)
   Lawd, have mercy on my soul, I think that now I hear you! (repeat)

Play and Play Piano Book for Beginners

Color the pictures of the old woman and the young man.

BASS CLEF

INSTRUCTIONS

Circle the Bass Clef sign below. The Bass Clef sign names the notes from Middle C on down the keyboard.

- The Bass Clef line 4 note name is **F**. The line is "Fire Engine Red" to help you remember **F**.
- The next note name going up the staff is **G**. It is above the **F** line and is in space 4.
- The next note name going up the staff is **A**. It is on the line 5 above the **G** space.

Find **F** on the keyboard with the fifth finger of your left hand. It is the F down to the left from Middle **C**. Your fourth finger will play **G** and your third finger will play **A**.

Play **F G A**.

Play **A G F**.

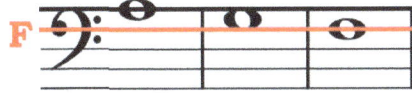

Circle the Bass Clef sign on the staff below.
Put finger 5 on F. Finger 4 will play G and finger 3 will play A.
The stems of the notes are going down to tell you to play with your left hand.
Play and sing the note names.

Play and Play Piano Book for Beginners

HOT CROSS BUNS

INSTRUCTIONS
Clap and read the rhythm.
Put your left hand finger 3 on A. Finger 4 will play G and finger 5 will play F.
Play and sing the letter names then play and sing the words.

Hot cross buns, Hot cross buns,

One a pen-ny, two a pen-ny, Hot cross buns.

FROG IN THE MEADOW

INSTRUCTIONS
Clap and read the rhythm.
Put your left hand finger 3 on A. Finger 4 will play G and finger 5 will play F.
Play and sing the letter names then play and sing the words.

Frog   in the   mea-dow,   Can't   get him   out.

Take a   lit-tle   stick and   stir   him a - bout.

Play and Play Piano Book for Beginners

CLOSET KEY

INSTRUCTIONS
Clap and read the rhythm.
Put your left hand finger 3 on A. Finger 4 will play G and finger 5 will play F.
Play and sing the letter names then play and sing the words.

I have lost the clos-et key in that lad-y's gar - den,

I have lost the clos-et key, in that lad-y's gar - den.

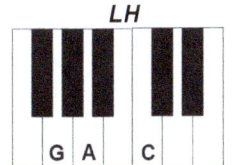

COBBLER, COBBLER

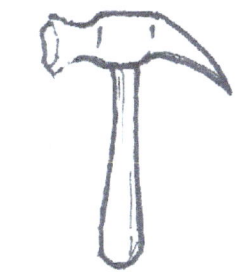

INSTRUCTIONS
Clap and read the rhythm.
Put your left hand thumb on Middle C.
Finger 3 will play A and finger 4 will play G.
Play and sing the note names then play and sing the words.

Cob-bler, Cob-bler, mend my shoe, Let it done by half past two.

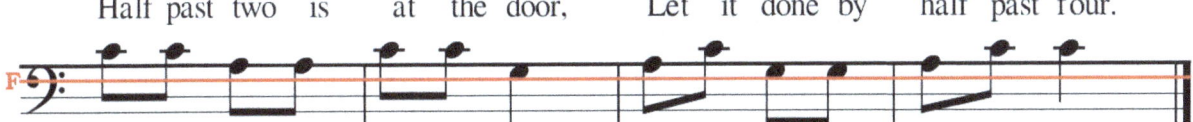

Half past two is at the door, Let it done by half past four.

Play and Play Piano Book for Beginners

BASS CLEF B

INSTRUCTIONS
Circle the new Bass Clef B in the patterns below. Play and sing the note names.

THREE OLD SONGS WITH BASS CLEF B-A-G

Here are three old songs that use the new Bass Clef B A G pattern.
Put your left hand finger 2 on B. Finger 3 will play A and finger 4 will play G.
Play and sing the note names then play and sing the words.

HOT CROSS BUNS

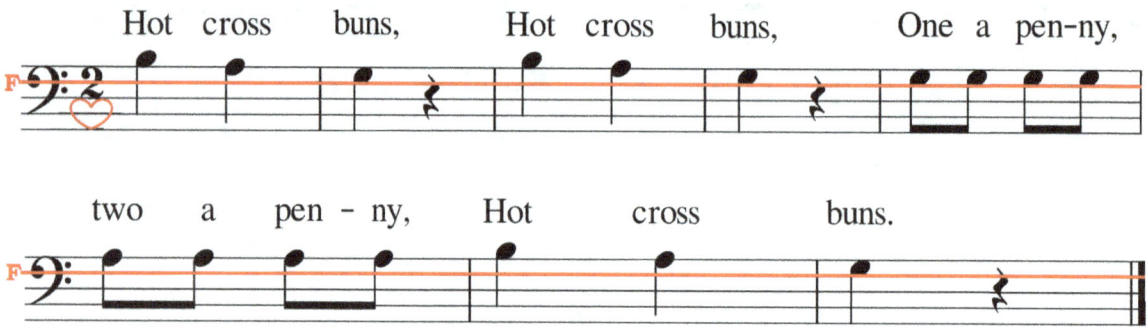

FROG IN THE MEADOW

Frog in the mea-dow, can't get him out. Take a lit-tle stick and stir him a-bout.

CLOSET KEY

I have lost the clo-set key, in that lad-y's gar-den.
I have lost the clo-set key, in that lad-y's gar-den.

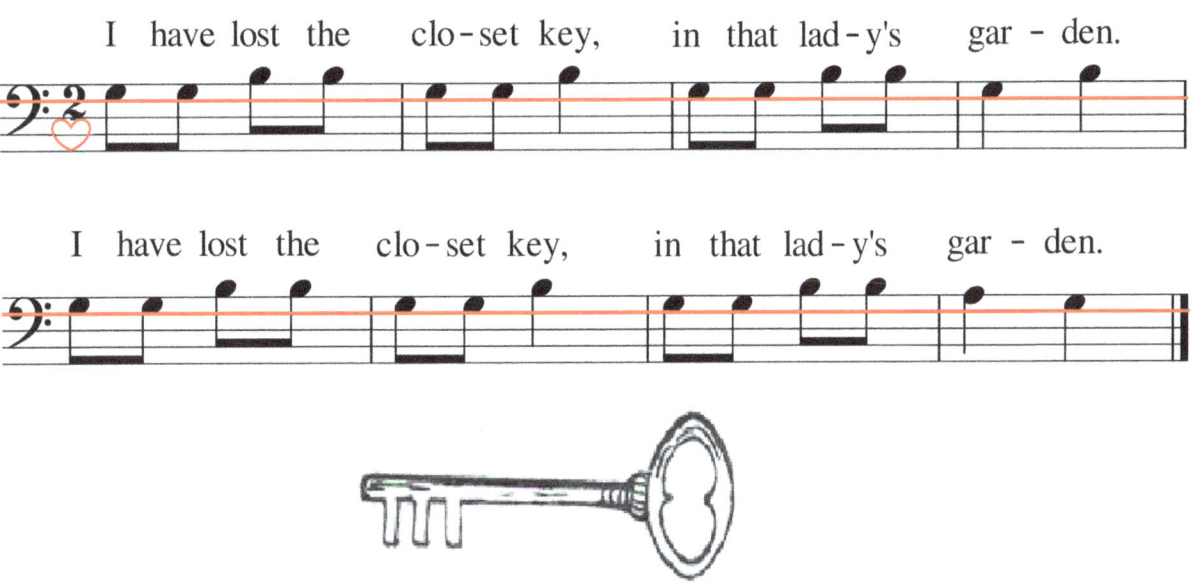

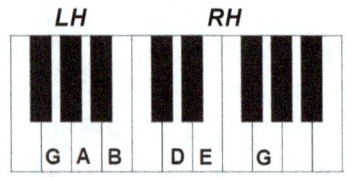

HOGS IN THE CORNFIELD

INSTRUCTIONS
Number the measures.
Sing the words and clap the rhythm.
Sing the rhythm names as you clap.
Put both thumbs on Middle C. Remember, the song begins at measure 1 in the Bass Clef.

Hogs in the corn field, cows in the clo - ver. Tell them

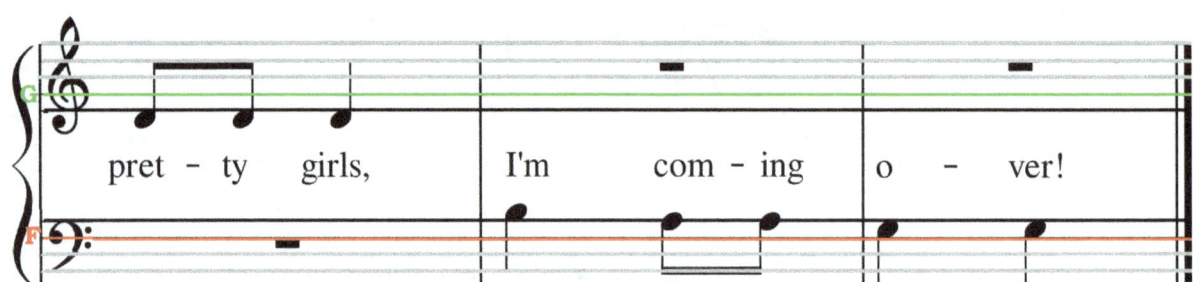

pret - ty girls, I'm com - ing o - ver!

OVER THE RIVER TO FEED MY SHEEP

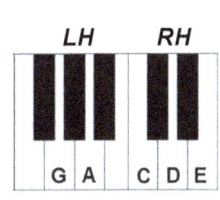

INSTRUCTIONS
Number the measures. Put both thumbs on Middle C.
Play and sing the rhythm then play and sing the words.

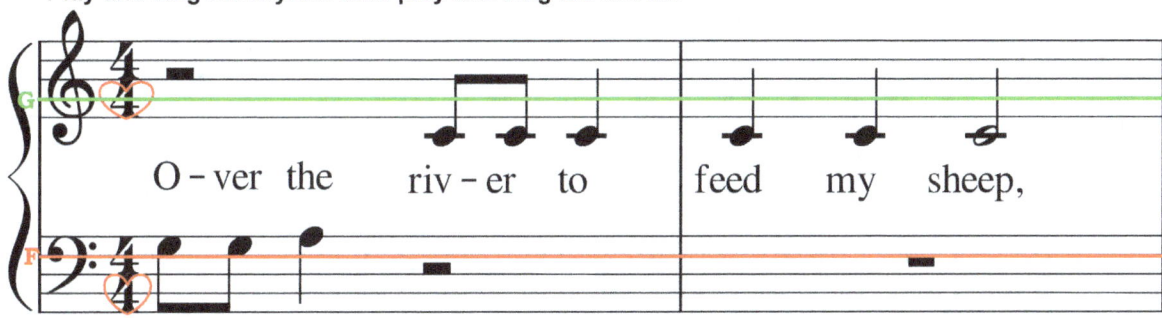

2. Tramplin' down the weavily wheat, tramplin' down the barley,
   Tramplin' down the weavily wheat, to bake a cake for Charlie.

3. Charlie is a fine young man, Charlie is a dandy,
   Charlie loves to go downtown to treat the girls to candy.

Play and Play Piano Book for Beginners

BOOTS OF SHINING LEATHER

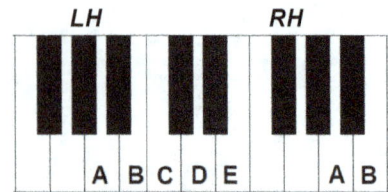

INSTRUCTIONS
Number the measures.
Put both thumbs on Middle C. Finger 5 of your right hand will stretch
  to play both A and B.
Play and sing the note names, then play and sing the words.
Play the song in a round with your teacher or another student.

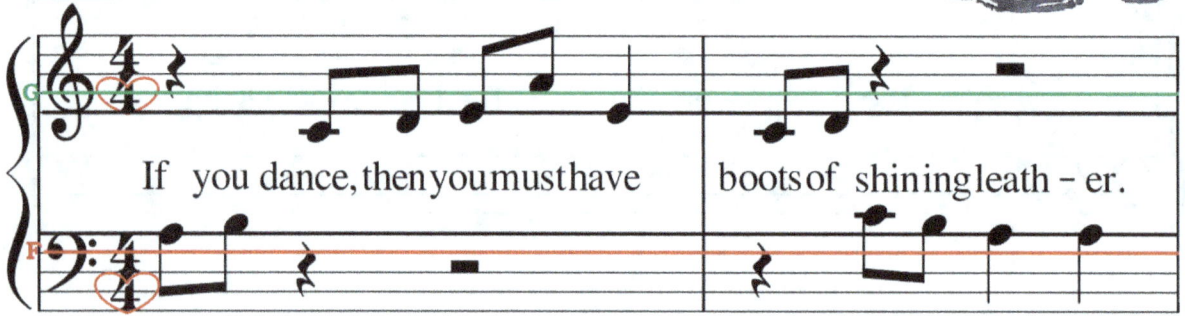

If you dance, then you must have boots of shining leath-er.

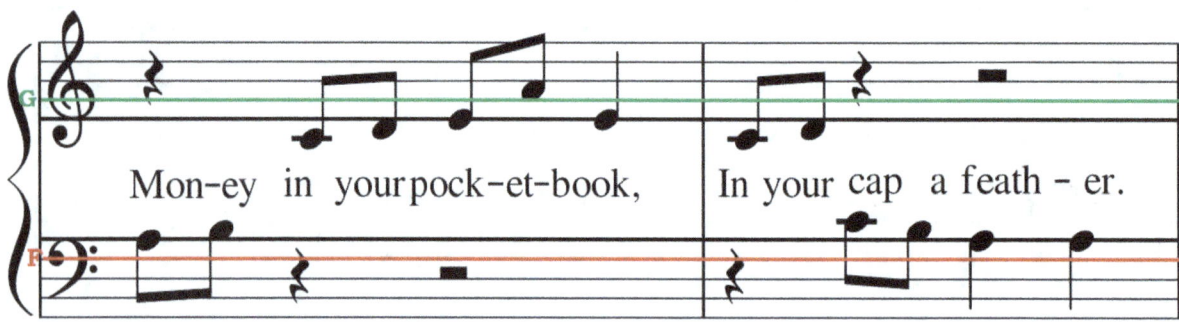

Mon-ey in your pock-et-book, In your cap a feath-er.

But if you would sing with me, You don't need a

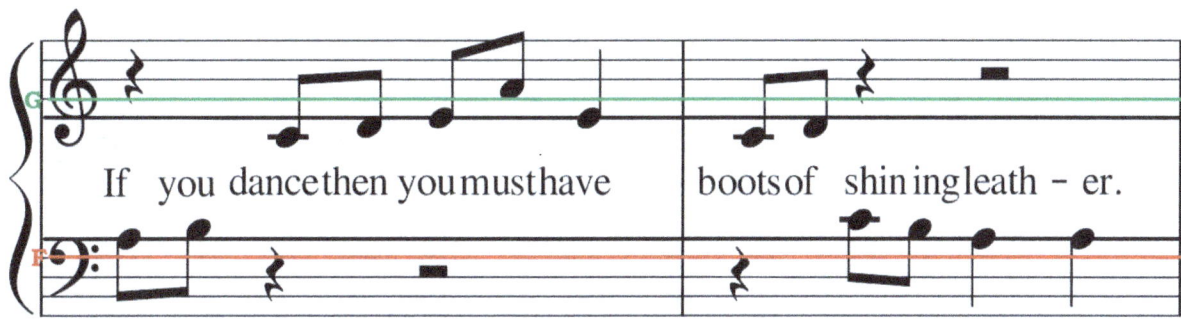

BUTTON, YOU MUST WANDER

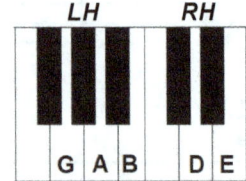

INSTRUCTIONS
Here is an old song to play on the Grand Staff.
Number the measures.
Put your Left Hand third finger on G. Put your Right Hand thumb on D.
Play and sing the note names, then play and sing the words.

But-ton you must wan - der, wan-der, wan-der,

3

But-ton you must wan - der ev - 'ry - where.

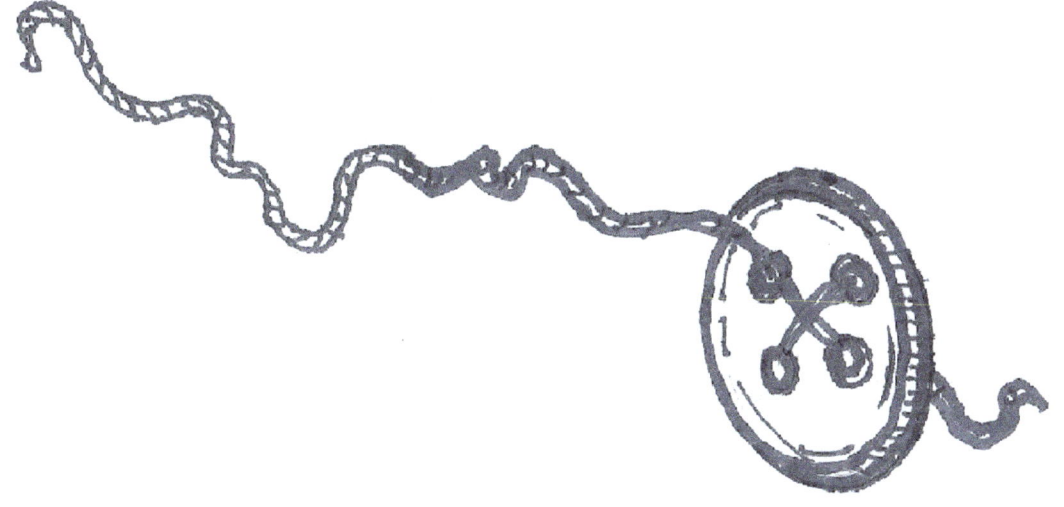

KING'S LAND

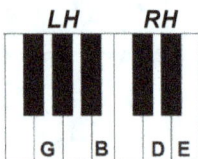

INSTRUCTIONS
Number the measures.
Circle the phrases in the words of the song.
Put both thumbs on Middle C.
Play and sing the rhythm names then play and sing the words.

I'm on the King's land, the King is not at home,

He's gone to Bos- ton to buy his wife a comb.

COME THROUGH 'NA HURRY

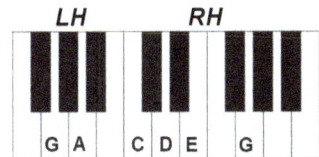

INSTRUCTIONS
Number the measures.
Circle the ti-ta-ti rhythm patterns in the song.
Circle the ti rests in measures 1 and 3.
Put both thumbs on Middle C.
Play and sing the rhythm names then play and sing the words.

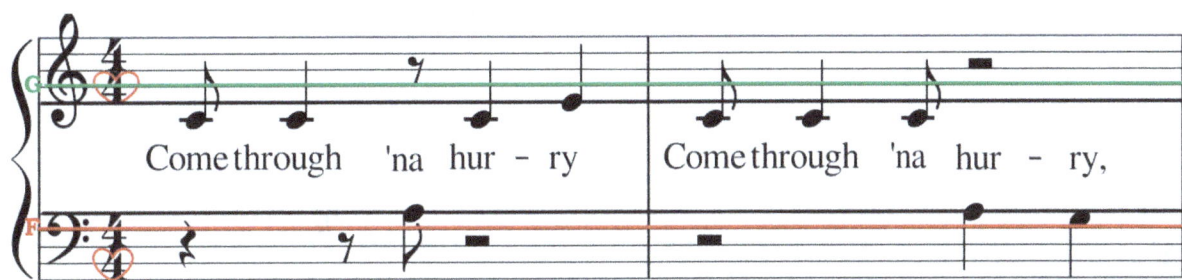

Come through 'na hur - ry Come through 'na hur - ry,

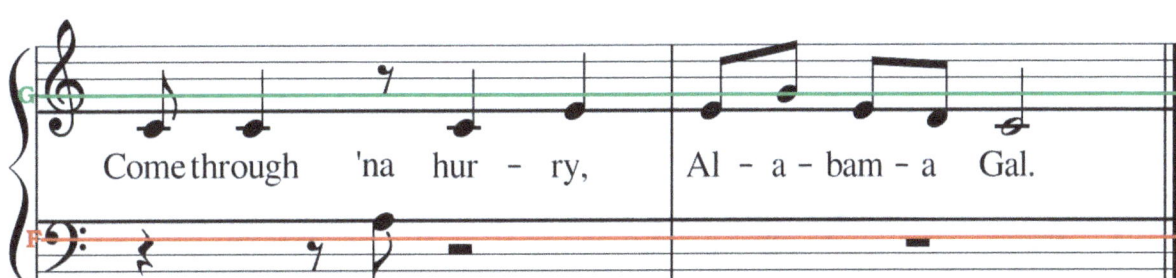

Come through 'na hur - ry, Al - a - bam - a Gal.

2. I don't know how, how,
   I don't know how, how,
   I don't know how, how,
   Alabama Gal.

3. I'll show you how, how,
   I'll show you how, how,
   I'll show you how, how,
   Alabama Gal.

4. Ain't I rock candy,
   Ain't I rock candy,
   Ain't I rock candy,
   Alabama Gal.

Play and Play Piano Book for Beginners

BIG FAT BISCUIT

INSTRUCTIONS
Number the measures.
Circle the tam-ti patterns.
Circle the ti-ta-ti pattern.
Circle the F#'s.
Put both thumbs on Middle C.
Play and sing the rhythm, then play and sing the words.

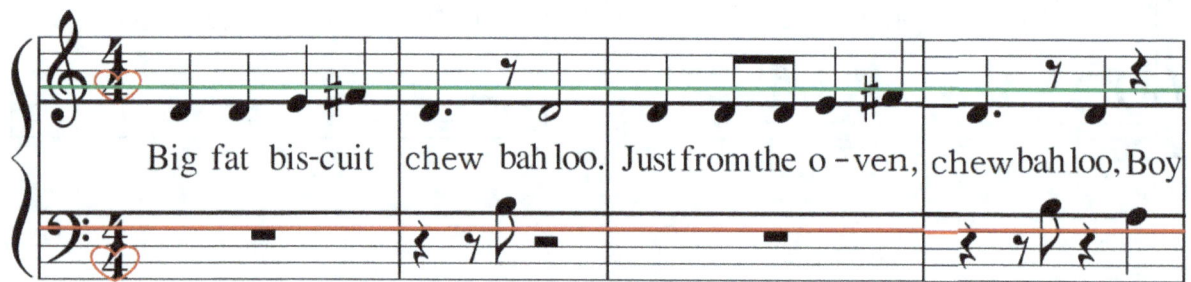

Big fat bis-cuit chew bah loo. Just from the o-ven, chew bah loo, Boy

Jump o - ver yon - der chew bah loo.

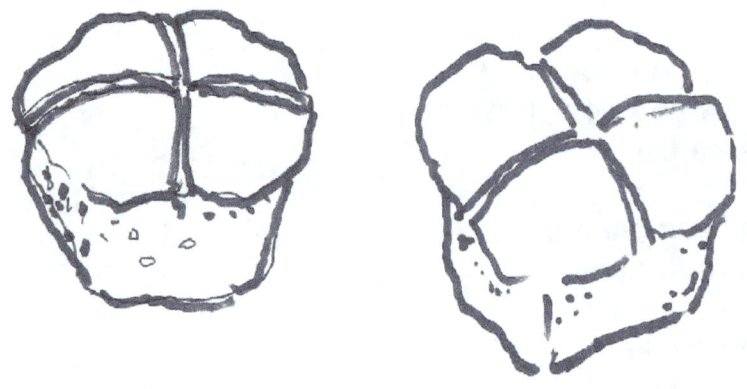

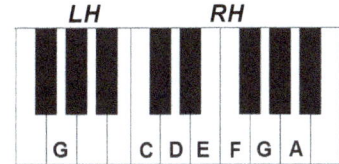

LONG ROAD OF IRON

INSTRUCTIONS
Number the measures. Look for the incomplete measure at the beginning of the song, then begin numbering after the barline.
Circle the tam-ti rhythms.
Put both thumbs on Middle C.
Play and sing the rhythm, then play and sing the words.

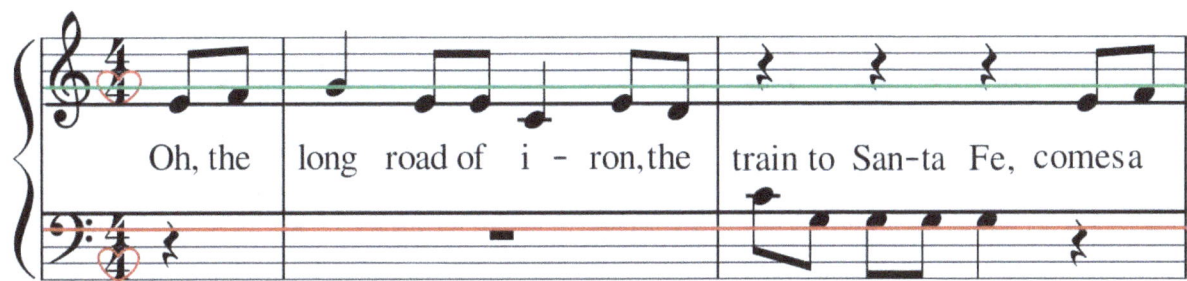

Oh, the | long road of i - ron, the | train to San-ta Fe, comes a

trav - lin' down the | track with a cheek-y, cheek-y | chay.

Play and Play Piano Book for Beginners

SKIP TO THE BARBER SHOP

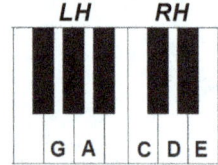

INSTRUCTIONS
Number the measures.
Circle the ti-ta-ti pattern in the song.
Circle the tam-ti pattern in the song.
Put both thumbs on Middle C.
Play and sing the rhythm names then play and sing the words.

Skip, skip to the bar-ber shop, I left my hat at the

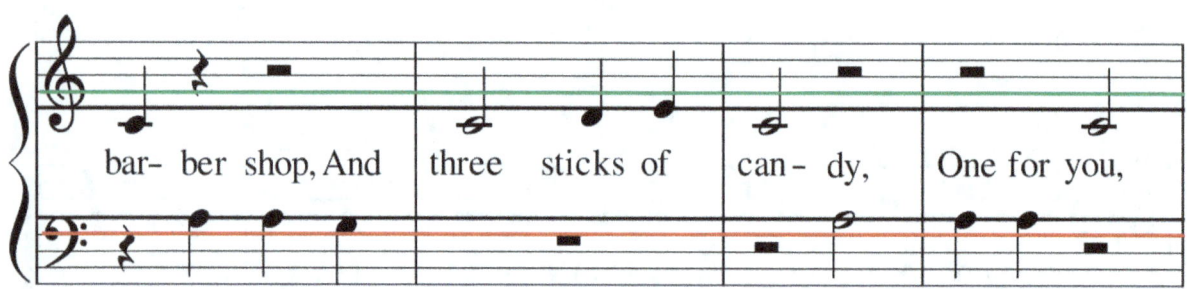

bar- ber shop, And three sticks of can - dy, One for you,

One for me And one for Sis - ter Sal - ly.

Student Edition

JUMP, FROG, JUMP

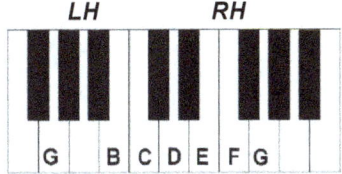

INSTRUCTIONS
Number the measures.
Circle the meter signature.
Put both thumbs on Middle C.
Play and count the rhythm. Remember to count 3 beats in each measure.
Play and sing the words.

Jump, frog, jump, the 'ga-tor is there; Jump, frog, jump and you will be spared!

Play and Play Piano Book for Beginners

O COME, ALL YE FAITHFUL

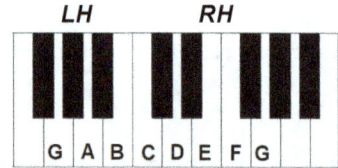

INSTRUCTIONS
Number the measures. Look for the incomplete measure at the beginning of the song then begin numbering after the bar line.
Circle the meter signature.
Circle the tam-ti rhythm patterns.
Play and sing the rhythm names then play and sing the words.

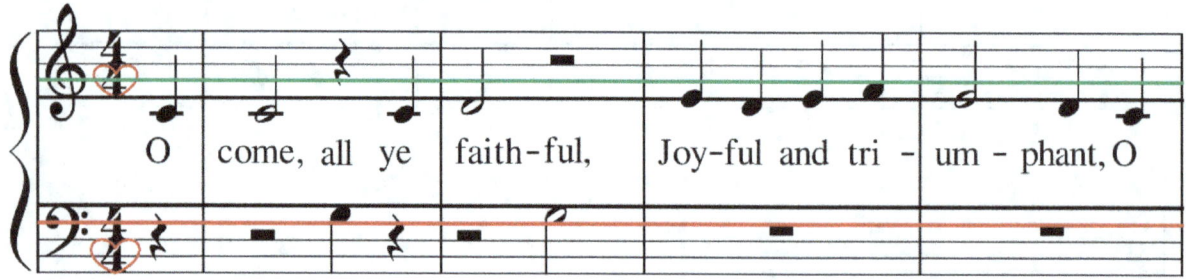

O come, all ye faith-ful, Joy-ful and tri - um - phant, O

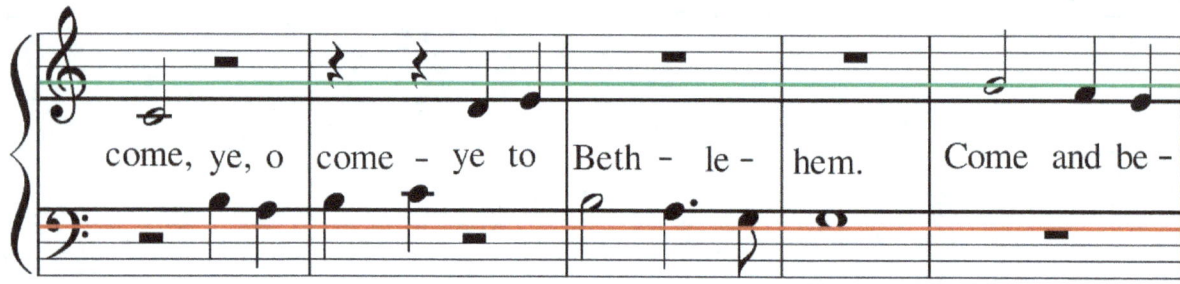

come, ye, o come - ye to Beth - le - hem. Come and be -

hold him, Born the King of an - gels. O come let us a -

Student Edition

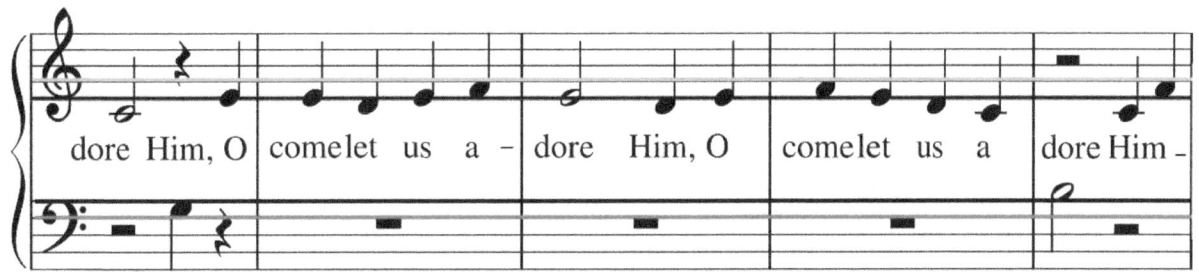

AMAZING GRACE

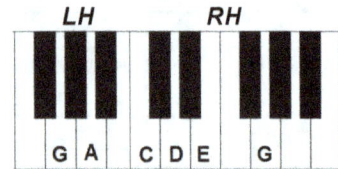

INSTRUCTIONS
Number the measures. Look for the incomplete measure at the beginning of the song then begin numbering after the bar line.
Circle the meter signature.
Circle the tam-ti rhythm patterns.
Play and sing the rhythm names then play and sing the words.

A - maz - ing grace! How sweet the sound, that

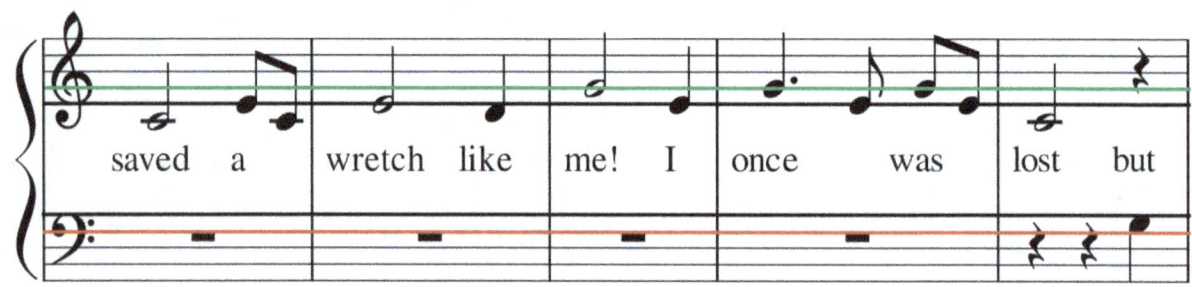

saved a wretch like me! I once was lost but

now - I'm - found; Was blind but now I see.

Alphabetical Listing of Pieces

Amazing Grace 74
Apple, Peach, Pear, Plum 10, 14
Bee, Bee Bumble Bee 15
Big Fat Biscuit 68
Boots of Shining Leather 62-63
Bounce High 9, 12, 28, 37
Button, You Must Wander 44, 64-65
Closet Key 17, 43, 56, 59
Cobbler, Cobbler 57
Come Through 'Na Hurry 67
Daddy Shot a Bear 45
Doggie, Doggie 20, 24
Ducks and Geese 27
Frère Jacques 50
Frog in the Meadow 18, 38, 41, 55, 59
Hogs in the Cornfield 60
Hop Old Squirrel 39, 42
Hot Cross Buns 40, 54, 58
I Climbed Up the Apple Tree 3
In and Out 7, 21, 25, 36
Johnny's It 34
Jump, Frog, Jump 71
King's Land 46, 66
Lemonade 26, 35
Long Road of Iron 69
Lucy Locket 13, 29
Nanny Goat 33
Naughty Kitty Cat 47
O Come, All Ye Faithful 72-73
Old Woman 51
Over the River to Feed my Sheep 61
Pease Porridge Hot 16
Plainsies, Clapsies 30, 37
Rain, Rain 11, 23
Ring Around the Rosie 48
Skip to the Barber Shop 70
Snail, Snail 8
We Are Dancing in the Forest 31
Who's That Tapping at the Window 49